GREEN BELT
SUDOKU™

Michael Rios

Sterling Publishing Co., Inc.
New York

CONTENTS

Introduction

3

Puzzles

5

Answers

155

4   6   8   10   9   7   5   3   2

Martial Arts Sudoku and Green Belt Sudoku
are trademarks of Sterling Publishing Co., Inc.

Published by Sterling Publishing Co., Inc.
387 Park Avenue South, New York, NY 10016
© 2005 by Michael Rios
Distributed in Canada by Sterling Publishing
c/o Canadian Manda Group, 165 Dufferin Street,
Toronto, Ontario, Canada M6K 3H6
Distributed in the United Kingdom by GMC Distribution Services,
Castle Place, 166 High Street, Lewes, East Sussex, England BN7 1XU
Distributed in Australia by Capricorn Link (Australia) Pty. Ltd.
P.O. Box 704, Windsor, NSW 2756, Australia

Sterling ISBN-13: 978-1-4027-4022-0
ISBN-10: 1-4027-4022-0

For information about custom editions, special sales, premium and
corporate purchases, please contact Sterling Special Sales
Department at 800-805-5489 or specialsales@sterlingpub.com.

INTRODUCTION

To solve sudoku puzzles, all you need to know is this one simple rule:

Fill in the boxes so that each of the nine rows, each of the nine columns, and each of the nine 3×3 sections contain all the numbers from 1 to 9.

And that's all there is to it! Using these simple rules, let's see how far we get on this sample puzzle at right. (The letters at the top and left edges of the puzzle are for reference only; you won't see them in the regular puzzles.)

	A	B	C	D	E	F	G	H	I
J									
K					2		1	8	4
L	9		5		7		2		6
M	1		4	3	9	2		7	
N				7		6			
O		7		1	4	8	9		2
P	3		2		6		8		5
Q	8	4	9		3				
R									

The first number that can be filled in is an obvious one: box EN is the only blank box in the center 3×3 section, and all the digits 1 through 9 are represented except for 5. EN must be 5.

The next box is a little trickier to discover. Consider the upper left 3×3 section of the puzzle. Where can a 4 go? It can't go in AK, BK, or CK because row K already has a 4 at IK. It can't go in BJ or BL because column B already has a 4 at BQ. It can't go in CJ because column C already has a 4 at CM. So it must go in AJ.

Another box in that same section that can now be filled is BJ. A 2 can't go in AK, BK, or CK due to the 2 at EK. The 2 at GL rules out a 2 at BL. And the 2 at CP means that a 2 can't go in CJ. So BJ must contain the 2. It is worth noting that this 2 couldn't have been placed without the 4 at AJ in place. Many of the puzzles rely on this type of steppingstone behavior.

We now have a grid as shown.

Let's examine column A. There are four blank boxes in column A; in which blank box must the 2 be placed? It can't be AK because of the 2 in EK (and the 2 in BJ). It can't be AO because of the 2 in IO. It can't be AR because of the 2 in CP. Thus, it must be AN that has the 2.

	A	B	C	D	E	F	G	H	I
J	4	2							
K					2		1	8	4
L	9		5		7		2		6
M	1		4	3	9	2		7	
N				7	5	6			
O		7		1	4	8	9		2
P	3		2		6		8		5
Q	8	4	9		3				
R									

By the 9's in AL, EM, and CQ, box BN must be 9. Do you see how?

We can now determine the value for box IM. Looking at row M and then column I, we find all the digits 1 through 9 are represented but 8. IM must be 8.

This brief example of some of the techniques leaves us with the grid at right.

You should now be able to use what you learned to fill in CN followed by BL, then HL followed by DL and FL.

As you keep going through this puzzle, you'll find it gets easier as you fill in more. And as you keep working through the puzzles in this book, you'll find it gets easier and more fun each time. The final answer is shown below.

	A	B	C	D	E	F	G	H	I
J	4	2							
K					2		1	8	4
L	9		5		7		2		6
M	1		4	3	9	2		7	8
N	2	9		7	5	6			
O		7		1	4	8	9		2
P	3		2		6		8		5
Q	8	4	9		3				
R									

This book consists of 300 puzzles of medium level of difficulty.

—Michael Rios

	A	B	C	D	E	F	G	H	I
J	4	2	1	6	8	3	5	9	7
K	7	3	6	5	2	9	1	8	4
L	9	8	5	4	7	1	2	3	6
M	1	5	4	3	9	2	6	7	8
N	2	9	8	7	5	6	4	1	3
O	6	7	3	1	4	8	9	5	2
P	3	1	2	9	6	7	8	4	5
Q	8	4	9	2	3	5	7	6	1
R	5	6	7	8	1	4	3	2	9

1

2

3

5		7			9			
		2				9		4
6		1	7			5		2
			6		4			
9				5				8
			9		7			
2		6			1	4		7
8		5				1		
			5			2		6

4

	1	6				7		
		7	9					
			7		4			1
	6		5		3		2	
	5			1			8	
	8		6		2		4	
9			2		6			
					9	2		
		8				3	9	

5

		8	6					
9				2	7			
1						5	6	4
		5	9	4				
	2	9		5		6	3	
			6	8	9			
2	1	7						3
			1	8				2
					2	1		

6

5		4			6			
					3			2
					5	3	8	
	5	7	8			9		
2			3	7	1			6
		8			2	4	1	
	1	6	5					
8			1					
			6			2		1

7

		3		8			7	5
			5		3			
	6		4	9				8
		1			9	3		7
3		9	7			6		
2				7	4		6	
			6		1			
6	1			5		8		

8

2	7		5					
8						4		6
		6			1	3		
		8		1		6		
	5			9			4	
		2		3		8		
		5	1			7		
7		9						4
					4		1	2

Puzzle 9

		4					2	
				3		8		1
	2				6		9	
		3		8	1			5
1				6				4
9			5	2		3		
	5		9				8	
4		8		5				
	7					5		

Puzzle 10

			3					5
		5				8		1
			1		6	9	7	
			7		3		9	
7		6				2		4
	3		9		4			
	4	3	8		7			
9		8				1		
6					5			

1 / 1

		5						
	4		3	8	9			
1	9				5			7
	2	1		3	6			
		3		2		1		
			7	9		2	8	
6			9				1	5
			6	4	3		9	
						7		

1 / 2

		4					6	
					5			
	1	9	2		6	8		
	6			7	8		5	9
5				3				2
1	3		5	9			8	
		5	7		1	6	4	
			8					
	2					5		

			3	1				4
3		4			5	7	1	
			2					8
	6		4					
2		7		9		4		5
					6		7	
5					3			
	4	3	1			2		7
7				2	8			

				4	5	7		
				3	6	2		
	5		1					3
	7		2					5
9	3			1			4	2
5					4		6	
7					1		8	
		5	8	2				
		8	6	7				

	4		3					9
		3		2	1			8
					8		3	6
2		6					5	
				6				
	3					2		4
7	9		2					
3			1	7		8		
5					4		9	

	9			7	3	2		
3					8	6		
		6		4		5		3
7					4			
			7		9			
			2					6
8		2		9		1		
		7	4					5
		3	1	8			4	

1					2			
		8	4			9	3	5
	4							
		3		9	4			7
9				3				8
2			1	6		3		
							7	
4	9	7			8	1		
			5					9

1					9		4	
6	7					5		2
	8	3				9		
			9		2		8	3
				1				
2	4		5		8			
		6				7	3	
8		7					2	9
	2		1					5

19

7					1			
			6	4				3
9	4	8						
		2		9	4	8	6	
	1						4	
	8	5	7	3		1		
						9	8	6
2				6	7			
			3					4

20

	8		6	5		3		
		2				9		
7		6		8				5
		1			5			
	6		9	3	7		8	
			2			5		
9				4		6		3
		8				1		
		4		2	1		7	

								6
	6				7			8
		8		1	7	5	3
	8			7	9	6		5
7		4	1	8			2	
1	7	8	2		5			
9			7				3	
2								

3	6		2					
4			1					8
2		5					1	3
			4	5				
	1	4				9	8	
				1	6			
9	4					5		2
8					7			1
					9		3	7

1				2				3	9
		5		1		6			
					8				5	4
	9	2							8	
	6								9	
	1							3	7	
2	7				5					
				6		7	5			
6	5				4					3

9					3					2
6				1				7		9
		8		5		9	1			
				8	1			4		
		3			4	6				
		5		2		1	3			
8		6				3				5
7					8					1

						3		9
8		4	6					
	3				4		6	
		1		4	8	2		7
	9						3	
3		8	1	7		4		
	1		4				8	
					7	1		3
5		2						

8			4	9				3
					5			2
					1		7	8
	4						5	
7	1		2		6		8	9
	9						3	
2	5		3					
1			7					
4				6	8			7

27

7	6	5			1			
						3		9
	1			4				
		7			9		6	3
		4	7	3	2	1		
2	5		1			4		
				1			3	
4		6						
			5			7	4	8

28

	2					9	6	7
								8
5	3				7			
9			6	7				
		7	1	8	4	6		
			5	2				1
			7				1	5
7								
6	1	8					2	

		1			6	4		3
		5			2		8	
					3		6	5
						3		4
	9	3				8	1	
5		8						
7	1		6					
	2		5			7		
8		4	3			9		

	4				3	6		
6			5	1		9		
7								
				9			1	2
9		4	6		1	7		5
2	3			8				
								6
		8		5	9			7
		7	1				4	

						5	4	
9	5		2					8
						2	1	3
			4	8		3		
	3	2		7		6	8	
		4		3	5			
2	4	5						
6					8		2	5
	1	7						

			2		3		9	
		6	7			3		
				9		7		4
				7	5	8		
5		9		1		4		7
		1	4	2				
9		2		5				
		4			6	2		
	5		1		2			

		8				2		
		7			1		6	
1			7		2			4
	5	4	3			9		
	7			2			1	
		9			7	4	8	
3			5		6			8
	9		1			7		
		1				3		

	1		3	4	7			
			1					
9					6			4
6	9					2	7	
3		5				9		8
	2	7					1	3
2			7					1
					5			
			4	6	2		5	

	1			4	9			5
8			1	7				
			5			7		6
4	8						9	
				3				
	2						5	4
6		4			8			
				2	4			9
7			9	5			8	

	6		9	1		2		3
3					2			
		7				9		
	4		8	2			9	
				6				
	3			7	5		6	
		8				6		
			1					9
7		4		5	3		1	

3 / 7

				8	7			
		1						3
	7		4	6	1			
8	9					6	1	
		4		2		7		
	5	2					3	8
			6	1	3		5	
2						9		
			2	7				

3 / 8

	3					1	2	
			8					
		1	2	9	6	3		
	8			7				9
	2	3				7	5	
7				6			3	
		6	1	8	4	5		
					7			
	1	4					8	

8					5	7		
6		1		7				
				1				8
2		4	3			8		5
	3						7	
7		9			8	1		4
4				9				
				2		5		1
		7	4					2

		9	2	3		4		
					8		1	
4			7			2		6
	9			5				
5			6		4			9
				7			6	
3		8			7			5
	7		1					
		6		2	9	7		

		8	9		2			6
1			4	8				
	9							
	2			4	9			5
	3	6		5		4	1	
5			2	1			8	
							3	
			3	7				9
7			6		1	8		

9	4						2	
7					6			
	1		7	8	4			
1		2					5	
		8		1		6		
	5					8		1
			2	5	1		7	
			6					9
	6						3	5

7			5	2	8	4		
3			1				8	
					9	5	6	
9	6					3		
		1					2	6
	4	3	8					
	9				3			2
		2	7	9	4			3

		4			2			
8		7		9		2		4
5			1				8	
		6	9	8				
4				2				8
				3	6	1		
	8				9			6
1		2		7		8		5
			5			3		

4·5

3	2				4	5	9	
				8			1	3
9								
	5			1	9			7
	4						6	
7			4	2			5	
								1
6	9			3				
	8	5	6				3	9

4·6

|
|---|

|
|---|

|
|---|

		9			8			7
5		1	9					
8		4		2				
1			7	8			3	
2				9				5
	8			5	2			1
				1		3		2
					5	1		6
6			3			4		

	7			6		1		
		1			9		4	
8				7		5	6	9
						7	3	
4								6
	5	3						
1	2	5		3				8
	6		8			3		
		7		4			2	

	5		4		3	8	7	
					2			
3		6		8				
		3			8	6		1
6								2
5		2	9			4		
				9		5		4
			1					
	6	9	8		5		3	

							6	
1		9			5		4	
		6	8	4	9	3	7	
			5			1		
			4	8	7			
		8			1			
	8	2	7	9	4	6		
	6		3			4		2
	3							

	6		4	8				
5		8				9		
			6		7		3	8
				7			8	1
	4						2	
1	3			6				
4	2		5		1			
		3				6		2
			9	6			1	

			5	6	7			1
						4		
	7	3	9			5		8
	1					8		
		5	3		2	1		
		2					6	
1		9			6	2	4	
		6						
4			2	8	5			

2	9			4				5
							7	
		3			5		9	4
	7		8					1
	6	5				9	2	
3					9		6	
6	3		7			2		
	5							
7				8			4	9

5 3

1	9				8			
						2		
5	4	2	9	6				
	8			7	2	3		
		1		4		9		
		4	8	5			1	
				8	1	4	5	3
		5						
			6				8	7

5 4

			8	3				1
4			2		6			
		2		1		8		
3			1	8				5
		1				3		
6				4	2			7
		7		6		4		
			4		1			3
5				7	8			

5

			7			6		
7		4		3	6	1	2	
						5		
			2		3	8		
8				4				9
		9	6		5			
		6						
	4	2	5	6		3		7
		8			4			

6

		6	8	5		2		4
		5	9	4				6
	4				5			9
6				7				5
9			1				8	
1				9	3	4		
2		4		6	7	8		

	8							2
9	6					5		
		4			6	7		
	9		6			3	2	4
				1				
5	2	6			9		1	
		9	5			6		
		3					9	1
1							3	

	1							6
8				2		5		9
	4		1				2	7
2		7			8			
	8			4			5	
			5			7		3
1	6				3		9	
9		8		5				4
4							6	

3						1		
	2	9	3	6				
	6			2				8
8		6	1	9				
		2				9		
			4	2	5			7
5			7				3	
			1	3	8	7		
		3						2

4	1	5						
8						3		7
			8			5	4	
			7			1	3	
	2			3			9	
	7	4			2			
	9	6			1			
2		7						5
						6	7	9

6
1

			4			1		
7	1					6		9
	3			5		7		
	9		6	3	4	8		
				9				
		4	2	8	1		9	
		7		6			3	
6		3					8	4
		8			2			

6
2

	9					1		
		5		6				9
		1	2				3	
5				4	1		9	
7			3		2			6
	3		6	5				4
	6				4	5		
9				7		2		
		7					6	

7		4				6		5
1					6	3		
			8	4				
9		2					6	
	6		2		8		7	
	4					5		9
				8	5			
		6	4					7
5		3				1		8

			9					
				7			1	
	5	1	4			6	7	
7				3	8		6	5
		4				2		
5	6		2	9				7
	1	2			7	5	8	
	8			6				
					1			

			4	7			2	8
9			6					
		7			1			3
	5					3		
	3	6	2		9	1	8	
		4					7	
8			1			2		
					8			6
5	6			4	3			

7					3	9		
4	5				1			8
	2				8	7	3	
			8		7			
	8						2	
			5		4			
	1	5	6				7	
8			7				5	9
		2	1					6

		4	1	9				8
			8		6		7	
6					7	4		
			6				9	
1	4			8			2	5
	9				5			
		3	9					2
	7		5		3			
5				2	1	7		

			9		6			
7	1			5		9		
	9	4	1					
		5			4		2	
	3	1		7		8	9	
	8		6			3		
					8	4	1	
		6		1			8	7
			4		2			

Puzzle 69

6			8			4	3	
			7	2		9	5	
	9			4				
	4					6		9
	3						4	
2		1					8	
				7			9	
	7	9		6	5			
	5	6			3			2

Puzzle 70

						6	1	7
	9				6	4		3
					1	2		
	5	1	2	8				
				3				
			9	7		1	5	
		2	7					
8		4	3				6	
7	6	5						

7/1

		4		1		9		8
					3			
	9		7			6		
9		3		4	2		5	
			9		5			
	5		1	3		4		6
		2			4		1	
			3					
1		7		8		3		

7/2

4			7			8		
			2	1	9			4
				4			3	7
	1	4	6					3
3					8	6	1	
2	5			8				
9			3	5	4			
		3			6			9

	7	9			6		5	
	8				1			2
6				5		9	7	
5	1			7				
				3			9	7
	6	8		4				9
4			2				3	
	9		5			6	2	

	2				5	4		
		8	3					
	6	1				8		
2	5		8	7				
9		3		2		6		8
				9	3		2	7
		5				1	4	
					8	7		
		9	4				8	

		4		9		1	6	
				6	7			
	6	8	1					
		6			4		3	
3	9						1	6
	4		5			2		
					1	8	4	
			4	5				
	2	1		7		5		

		8		5			4	
	7			6				
	5	1		4	2		3	
1						9	7	
7								5
	4	6						1
	9		1	3		4	2	
				8			5	
	3			7		1		

7 / 7

	7			2			4	1
						8	3	
	3			1	7	5	9	
			6					5
8								3
9					5			
	9	7	1	5			2	
	8	5						
4	2			9			5	

7 / 8

				6		5		
1			8	5			7	6
			1		4		9	8
	3				9			
2								1
			3				6	
7	4		5		2			
3	5			8	1			4
		1		3				

43

	5				3	1		9
	8							6
	9		7	2				
		1	8				4	2
				6				
3	4				7	5		
				1	4		9	
7							2	
6		9	5				1	

	8	2		1	9	7		
6								
9		4			5		3	
				1	2	8	3	
3	2	8	5					
	7		8			3		9
								6
		9	6	3		1	5	

Puzzle 8-1:

			1				6	8
		6						
	2	7	6		4			
	3				6	5		9
6			7	2	9			4
1		9	3				7	
			2		8	6	4	
						1		
3	5				1			

Puzzle 8-2:

						4	6	7
		4						9
5				9		3		1
		8			3	6	1	4
				2				
7	1	6	4			5		
8		9		3				5
1						9		
2	5	7						

	2	8		4			3	
	1	7			6	5		4
3	4							
				8	3			
		3		2		9		
			6	9				
							8	7
5		4	9			2	1	
	7			1		4	5	

2		8			4		5	
	5			9	3	7		
7		9						
6	4	7			1			
			4			6	2	3
						5		6
		2	8	3			1	
	1		7			9		2

9			6	3				5
	3				2		9	8
	2		1		8		3	
						7		
			2	4	9			
		3						
	9		8		7		1	
4	8		9				5	
1				5	3			6

		2			3	6	5	
	1		4					
5					9			
8		1		9		2	3	
4				6				7
	2	3		7		4		5
			9					2
					1		4	
	3	4	7			9		

				2	8	9		
9			7				2	
7				5			6	8
1	2							6
	4						7	
3							8	1
8	5			9				3
	7				3			5
		1	4	7				

			3	2				8
2		8						
	4	7		5			9	
	7	2	8			9		4
9		6			4	3	5	
	9			1		8	6	
						7		3
8				3	7			

1					2		3	
5	6	7		4		8		
8	2						4	
			5					
		1	3	9	8	6		
				4				
	3						8	7
		6		7		3	5	4
	7		2					1

					6			
		9	3	1			2	
	7	6						1
	2	7			3		4	
		4	7	9	1	8		
	6		4			5	3	
6						3	1	
	5			2	4	6		
			6					

9	7				3	1		
	6		8			4		
2							8	
	5		3		6	2		
	1			8			6	
		2	9		4		1	
	2							3
		5			2		7	
		3	1				2	5

					5		9	8
			1				7	5
				8	2		3	
	7	3				6		4
			3		1			
6		9				8	5	
	6		8	1				
5	3				9			
8	9		2					

			1			2		4
					9		1	
4				8		3		7
					7	5	8	3
		5		1		9		
3	2	9	5					
8		3		9				6
	9		6					
6		2			4			

	6		4				3	7
		7		3			6	
						9	1	5
		3		5				
4	7			9			2	1
				4		7		
7	5	9						
	4			8		2		
1	2				7		4	

				6		5		
		4			2	3	8	
				4			1	7
9		6	8				7	
		3				2		
	8				1	6		9
1	4			7				
	7	5	2			1		
		8		1				

7			3			5		
9		8			7	6		3
	6	1						9
	7			9				4
5				8			6	
4						2	1	
8		5	2			4		6
		9			1			5

	9	6		4	8		5	7
4							3	
			7		3		2	
					2	3		6
5		9	4					
	3		8		4			
	6							5
1	5		6	9		2	4	

3					8	4		7
		7						2
1					3			
	4		1		2	5	9	
		1		8		3		
	6	3	4		9		2	
			3					8
8						6		
6			5	8				3

			5	3		7		1
		7			4		2	
4			1				9	
2				5			1	
	4			6			8	
	7			2				4
	3				5			8
	2		7			1		
8		5		9	6			

9	4	6		5				
					1		5	2
							4	
		7		4		3		8
	2		7	8	5		1	
4		1		9		5		
	9							
6	7		8					
				1		2	7	9

4					6	9		
8	9							
3		2	5		9		4	
				1	3			2
			9		7			
6			4	8				
	1		3		5	7		4
							1	8
		5	1					6

		4		7	9	1	3	6
						2		5
		6			2			
	6		2	4				
	9						5	
				9	1		7	
			1			4		
5		3						
7	1	8	4	3		5		

103

			9		2			7
2				4	6	8		
6			8	3			2	
1		5						
		9				2		
						5		1
	2			8	5			9
		4	1	2				6
7			6		4			

104

			5					
				8	6			3
2					3	1	7	6
		9					6	
8	3	7				9	4	1
	2					3		
9	1	2	3					4
5			9	7				
					2			

105

7		5		2		8	1	
						3		5
	1				7			
	7				5			2
	3		2	7	4		6	
1			6				3	
			5				9	
3		1						
	2	9		3		6		1

106

4	3	9	2					
			3			4	5	9
			4					8
		7						
3		1	8	4	7	9		2
						1		
1					3			
2	7	8			4			
					8	5	2	6

107

				9				
3	6	2	7		4			
	5						6	
5	2				9	1		4
	1						7	
9		7	6				2	5
	7						8	
			4		7	5	1	6
				1				

108

8	9		7			1		3
						4	8	
1		4						
		3		1	6		7	
	5						2	
	1		3	5		9		
						7		9
	2	7						
4		9			1		6	8

3		1	6		8		5	
4			3		5		8	
		8					7	
					3			
	1	9				3	4	
			7					
	6					9		
	3		4		2			7
	7		1		9	4		6

		1			6	4		5
		5					9	
		8		4	5	7		
5	2							
7		9				1		2
							7	8
		4	3	7		2		
	3					6		
1		2	6			9		

113

4	8				7		2	
2	6			8			5	
		7				9		4
			2					
		8	3		6	1		
					1			
7		1				2		
	4			5			1	3
	3		4				7	6

114

					6			
	3				2	7		8
			5	3			2	
2	9				5	1		
1	4						6	2
		8	3				5	4
	7			4	8			
3		1	2				7	
			6					

Puzzle 115:

					5			1
		3		6	4		9	
	9		3	7			8	
8							6	2
	3						1	
5	6							4
	2			4	3		7	
	5		2	1		6		
9			7					

Puzzle 116:

			8					
	8	6		7	3			9
	1	3	5				2	
		5					1	
		7		2		4		
	6					8		
	7				2	6	5	
3			1	9		2	8	
					4			

					4	1		
				7		3		5
9		7		3				
7		4		2			9	
		6	7		1	8		
	8			5		7		1
				9		4		2
3		8		6				
		9	2					

		1		4				
7		6						
4	5	9			7			
	7				4		3	8
		5	3		9	7		
6	4		5				2	
			6			8	7	5
						6		9
				9		2		

	2	6	3		1			8
	8				9	1	3	
	9					7		
2		7		5		6		9
		1					4	
	4	5	1				6	
7			9		4	5	8	

	9		8				2	
	7	3						1
	2			4			5	
	1			3	2	6		
		2				3		
		6	5	9			1	
	5			2			8	
2						7	9	
	8				1		3	

			2	5			9	
2				8	6		4	
8					9	6		
		9				5	1	
4				7				6
	2	1				3		
		2	5					8
	4		3	9				5
	3			6	2			

3						6	1	
4							8	3
1			4	7				9
	4		5	8				
	9			6			5	
				2	9		7	
7				1	8			5
9	3							2
	2	1						7

	1						8	5
8	5					7		
					4	9		2
		8			7		4	
	6			3			7	
	3		2			5		
9		5	1					
		7					6	8
6	8						5	

3	8	5			2			
7			1					
	1			9		4		
6			7					
9	2		3		1		7	6
					6			9
		7		6			9	
					3			5
			5			8	6	2

1 2 5

	6		2	9				
	2					6		
5	7			6	8	3		9
3				4	9			
				2				
			1	8				2
4		7	9	3			8	6
		8					7	
				7	6		4	

1 2 6

		4			5			1
6	9		2					
				4				3
		6		9		7	1	
	3		7		4		6	
	2	7		6		9		
7				8				
					7		2	8
2			1			3		

4		2						
		8	2	4			1	7
				8				9
3					5			
5	4		7	1	3		9	8
			9					6
9				7				
1	8			5	2	9		
						6		4

4			7					3
	3	7		8	9			6
		1			6			2
							7	
		2	8		3	1		
	1							
7			4			8		
1			9	6		4	3	
5					8			1

129

1			4				3	
	8					5		2
	5		3	7				1
		8		5	7			4
				3				
2			9	8		7		
3				9	1		8	
5		7					4	
	1				2			3

130

				3	9			
		8				3	5	
3			2		7		4	
8			1		3			7
		4				2		
7			9		2			5
	9		7		1			4
	2	6				1		
			6	2				

131

		2				7		
			9				4	6
1	6			7	8	3		
			8				1	5
			2		4			
8	3				7			
		9	3	2			6	7
5	2				9			
		1				9		

132

		3	2	5				1
							6	
	6		8	1	9			
3						1	2	
	4	1		8		6	7	
	2	8						3
			9	2	8		4	
	8							
9				6	1	2		

					2			8
		9	8					
		5	4	6	7		9	
4			5				1	
	1	8		2		5	3	
	5				4			2
	6		2	1	9	8		
					8	4		
9			6					

				8	6			5
8	3					9		2
		6					8	
7		1		6				3
	2			4			7	
4				5		2		1
	1					5		
2		4					1	7
6			3	1				

Puzzle 135

2					1	8		6
	4		2		6			
		6				5	7	2
		7						3
	9			4			5	
3						2		
5	3	1				6		
			1		8		3	
8		4	3					1

Puzzle 136

				1		7		
		6		4			9	1
2				8	5		4	
	6	7					1	
		1				3		
	2					8	5	
	5		4	7				6
1	7			3		2		
		8		9				

137

		6		1	5		3	
		1	4			2		9
3			2				5	
		2						
		8	6		4	3		
						1		
	8					1		2
5		9			2	4		
	4		5	7		8		

138

		9	7				3	5
2							7	
	7	6		9	1			4
	1	2		5				
				2		5	1	
1			9	3		8	6	
	3							1
6	4				7	3		

139

3	9				8		6	
		2		9		7		
	8				1			
1		5					7	6
			3		7			
4	7					5		2
			4				9	
		1		2		6		
	6		9				2	7

140

			7					
					2	5	3	
6		8	5			9		
3	5			4		7	1	
	8						9	
	9	1		6			5	4
		5			8	4		1
	7	4	2					
					4			

9		8		4	2	5		
	2				8			4
	5			9		1		
	7					4		
			3	6	7			
		9					7	
		4		8			6	
6			9				5	
		2	6	5		8		1

	1						9	2
			7	9	6			
			2		6		4	
		7				5		4
4				6				8
8		9				7		
	9		5		8			
		8	4	1				
3	2						5	

1				4				3
5	2							
		9	7		2			1
			9				8	5
		5	8	7	1	9		
4	9				5			
3			4		7	8		
							5	6
2				8				4

3								
	2	6	4			1	8	
		1			7		2	5
	9		7					
2				6				1
					8		3	
5	8		3			6		
	3	7			1	2	9	
								4

			8			2		4
			5					6
2		8					7	9
		4		3			5	8
		7		8		9		
8	6			1		4		
7	9					6		5
6					3			
3		1			9			

					5		7	
		6				5	4	
		7	3					8
1					7	6		
		3	2	5	6	9		
		8	1					2
7					3	1		
	6	1				8		
	5		7					

1 4 7

	7			1			8	
	9	3				4	6	
			6	5	3	7		
5					9	1		
				8				
		6	2					3
		8	5	9	2			
	5	1				9	7	
	6			4			2	

1 4 8

					2			3
6	9			1		2	8	
							4	
		1		2	8		3	
	3	6		5		8	9	
	5		6	7		1		
	8							
	6	9		8			5	1
7			5					

3			7			8	1	
	4		9					
	8		6			7		9
	3				8			1
5								2
9			5				6	
2		9			4		3	
					5		8	
	5	4			9			7

1	5	9					7	
6	2							
		3	7				2	
		2		1			8	
			4	5	6			
	3			8		5		
	8				4	7		
							3	9
	7					1	5	4

151

7	8			1		4		6
		1				3	8	
				8				
9	5							7
	7		8	5	1		9	
6							3	2
				9				
	3	2				9		
1		5		6			7	3

152

	4					9		1
			8	6		2	3	4
5			9					
	6	4	1				8	
	7				8	4	2	
					2			3
7	8	9		3	1			
1		3					9	

80

					8	7	5	
3	2		1					
	6	7						
	8	1			3	9		4
			7		1			
5		3	2			6	1	
						3	2	
					6		4	5
	3	9	8					

Puzzle 154

3		7	1				2	
9			6			1		
				5	3			
	7		2	9				
		8	5		1	7		
				3	6		8	
			4	2				
		5			9			4
	1				5	3		9

		7			1		6	
6			7	8			1	
8				4		3		5
		9	1					
5								6
					2	7		
3		4		9				1
	1			2	3			9
	9		6			5		

5	6	8	9				4	1
		7					8	3
	4							
3				7		9		
			5		1			
		2		8				6
							1	
9	3					5		
7	1				5	4	2	9

7	5	4		8				1
		6						
9		2			7			
8	9			7			5	
	2			1			6	
	4			3			8	9
			8			3		2
						6		
3				5		8	1	7

8	3							
7					9			
5		2	7				3	
	5			1			6	
1			8	4	5			9
	4			9			5	
	2				3	7		4
			9					3
							2	5

			4		9	3	7	
1		9	6					4
		4	5				9	
		2			4			
7								3
			7			8		
	4				8	9		
2					5	1		6
	8	6	1		2			

9		2	8					1
	5							
	4	6		1	5			2
			5			3		
	7		1	9	8		6	
		9			3			
7			2	5		6	1	
							9	
3					9	5		4

	3		6				5	
				9	1			
	6	7				4		
5		8		3			4	
4			1		2			5
	1			8		2		7
		5				1	6	
			8	5				
	4				9		3	

	5		3			8		4
1	2						6	5
					6			
					9	3		8
6			4		1			7
5		1	8					
			7					
4	1						7	9
9		5			4		3	

	1							
4	7		5	3		2	1	
		8		2		4	6	
			1		5		3	
	5		4		9			
	6	3		5		7		
	4	9		1	7		2	3
							8	

			8		1	9		3
2		1						6
			4			5		
4							3	
	8	9	7		5	4	2	
	2							5
		3			9			
6						3		4
8		4	6		3			

9		4					6	
		3	4	6			1	
		1	7			3	4	
6	7							
		9				7		
							8	3
	3	2			1	4		
	4			3	7	2		
	9					5		6

			8	4				
		1			3		8	
	6	8			1		5	
6		4				5	1	
			7		4			
	3	5				9		2
	5		1			4	9	
	1		4			2		
				6	7			

Puzzle 167

	6					9	5	
				6	2	4	3	
								6
7		6			4	1		
	3		2		1		8	
		2	5			7		3
6								
	2	1	3	8				
	4	8					2	

Puzzle 168

	4	9						
				8	5			
3				7	2	4		1
		6		3		9		2
2				1				8
4		1		9		6		
5		7	8	4				6
			6	2				
						1	2	

5				1				4
		1		2	3			6
					4	7	9	
9		5					7	
		2				5		
	7					1		8
	5	9	6					
4			2	9		3		
8				3				5

	4				6		8	
	7	6	1					
8	5	1				7		
				6	7		2	
	3			5			7	
	6		3	4				
		3				2	4	5
					3	8	1	
	9		8				3	

	7			4		5		9
			2					
	1			6	8	2		
	8	2		1				3
	3						5	
9				7		1	2	
		4	8	9			7	
					5			
1		8		2			3	

	5							
6	9			4	8			1
		2			9		6	4
4		3		7				
			9	1	3			
				2		7		5
7	1		2			4		
8			6	3			1	2
							5	

173

9					3	5	4	
			5	4			9	
5			8					6
2	3			1				
		7				1		
				5			2	8
1					4			2
	8			3	6			
	9	4	1					3

174

9	2	3		5	1		7	
6	1				7		4	
7								8
	5	6				1	9	
1								5
	3		8				5	4
	8		5	7		9	3	2

		6	2					3
		1			5		4	
		4		1	3	6		
		7	3					9
9								1
3					2	7		
		5	1	7		9		
	7		8			4		
8					6	2		

	1							9
2			7	1				
		5	4		6			7
				6	3	4	7	5
				5				
5	6	2	9	7				
9			8		2	1		
				3	7			2
3							5	

	9	3						
		5				8		
6			7				3	4
		9	2	7	4			
7			1		6			8
			5	3	8	2		
3	1				2			9
		8				3		
						6	5	

	5						1	
8	9					6		
6	4	7		8				
	6	2	8	1		7		
				5				
		8		6	4	5	2	
				7		1	9	5
		6					7	3
	1						8	

			1					4
6	5		4		8	7		
						3		
7	1			4		9		
	4		2		3		7	
		6		9			8	3
		2						
		5	3		4		6	8
1					5			

8			5		3		7	
3							2	8
					6			1
	5	6		1				
1			3		4			2
				7		1	8	
4			6					
6	3							5
	1		9		2			7

		5	4		6			
					1	9		
3						8		2
7		4		2	9			5
	6						1	
5			8	6		4		7
1		8						4
		9	6					
			5		2	1		

8				3	7			4
3						7	8	
9				8				
		4					2	9
			1	5	2			
7	2					3		
				2				3
	7	5						8
1			5	7				6

9	8		7			4	1	3
5	3				9		2	
	7				6			
			9			8		
				4				
		2			7			
			6				8	
	1		5				7	6
7	6	8			2		3	4

	6	4	5				8	
		8					9	
	7				8	3	4	
		2			3	5		
7								3
		6	2			4		
	9	5	1				7	
	2					8		
	4				2	1	5	

	1	4					5	
8		9	2		4			
		2		9				
		5	4		7			
		8	3		6	7		
			9		5	6		
				6		5		
			7		3	4		9
	3					1	2	

	9			3	1			
5		4			6			7
								8
		2		9			3	5
3			5		7			2
6	8			4		1		
2								
1			6			7		3
			2	1			8	

	4				7	8	2	
5				6	2			
1			8					
	8				3	5		7
	3						9	
9		6	2				1	
					1			2
			9	2				4
	9	2	5				3	

5					7		6	
					5	7		3
9			3		8		2	
	9					2		4
4				9				1
1		2					5	
	1		2		3			7
3		9	5					
	4		6					8

	7			2				3
							9	
2		1		9	3			
5	3	4	2			8		
				7				
		2			5	1	3	6
			6	4		7		1
	1							
4				5			2	

9				6		8	7	
	3	7	4					
			9			5		
	5		3		9			
		9		1		2		
			8		7		4	
		6			5			
					4	1	5	
	8	2		3				6

	7	6						
		4	1			7	2	
			5				4	9
	9		3					8
2			6		9			7
5					2		6	
7	1				6			
	2	3			5	4		
						8	1	

		5			9	4	1	
	6					8	7	5
7		2			4			
		3	2					
			9	4	1			
					7	6		
			7			5		8
4	3	7					9	
	5	6	4			1		

2			5			6	3	
1	7							4
				7	8	5		
					4		6	
5			1		9			8
	2		3					
		9	6	4				
7							5	6
	6	8			5			3

3					2			
4			7				3	2
	2				1		7	9
1					9			5
		2		6		8		
8			3					1
9	3		5				1	
6	7				8			4
			6					8

			5		9	8	6	2
8					7			
			3					
6		5		2		7		
	3	8				5	1	
		9		6		2		4
					1			
			4					9
7	2	4	9		6			

		4			5		1	2
		1					8	
		2			7	3		
		7					3	9
	1			2			5	
8	3					7		
		8	1			5		
	2					6		
6	4		9			2		

		6	5	1				
		8	4	2	7		1	
2								
4						3		
1		2	9		5	4		8
		3						6
								7
	4		2	5	3	8		
				9	8	1		

		9		1	3			2
	5						9	
			8	5			4	
3	1				4			
8	2						3	9
			8				1	6
	8		4	7				
	9						7	
7			3	6		2		

1		4		5		8		
9			4					
7		5	8			9		
6		2			3			
	1						3	
			1			2		6
		9			6	4		2
					8			5
		8		2		1		3

6	8			5	4			
						4		1
9			7	6				
2						1		8
		1	4	9	6	2		
5		3						9
				7	5			4
1		8						
			6	8			2	5

201

			4					1
	3	5	2					
8	4			5			6	
	5			4			3	
1		8				9		7
	9			7			2	
	2			1			7	5
					2	4	8	
7					5			

202

	7			5				2
4			1		6			
		2	9				4	6
			8				9	
2	9						5	1
	3				9			
6	2				1	4		
			2		5			3
7				3			6	

3		6	8	4				
1			5		2	4		
					9			
			7	8				
	6	4		9		7	1	
				5	6			
		9						
		8	1		4			2
				6	8	1		5

			9	5				
7		8						5
	1		2			9		8
	5			7	4		8	1
				3				
6	8		5	9			4	
5		9			3		1	
4						3		6
				6	9			

205

9	7				4			8
		2			1			
	3		6					
		5		1		4	6	
1		9				7		3
	4	7		3		8		
					2		4	
			5			6		
5			4				1	9

206

	1	8					2	
	5		2			7		
	4		1					3
	3					9	5	
		1	5	8	9	4		
	9	4					6	
1					4		7	
		7			6		8	
	6					3	4	

7		2	5		8			
			1				4	5
					3		2	8
	4				6			2
8				3				9
3			2				8	
5	8		4					
4	9				2			
			9		1	4		7

			8	4		7		
					5			1
	5					8	6	
8	3					6		
5	9		2		6		8	4
		6					5	9
	6	4					3	
1			4					
		8		1	2			

209

	2							
			6	7		3		
9						4	5	8
	1	2			5	9		4
		8		2		1		
3		9	8			5	6	
5	8	4						9
		1		8	7			
							1	

210

			7					
3		8	1					5
				6	5	8	1	
1					6	3		
		5	3			4	7	
		3	9					6
	1	4	6	2				
5						3	6	4
				7				

211

3		9				2		
			1				8	
	1			7	3			4
	8	5			9	1		
1								9
		6	8			7	4	
8			4	1			3	
	7				6			
		1				5		7

212

6			7	2			8	
					4	7	6	
5				8			9	
					7	9		
1		7				2		6
		5	6					
	5			9				7
	2	4	1					
	8			7	2			1

2 1 3

2		9			7	1		
	8	1		5			7	
		6	2	1		9		
								9
			5	3	4			
1								
		2		7	3	8		
	9			8		2	1	
		5	4			3		7

2 1 4

	9		4		2	1		
		7					6	2
6			1					8
		9	3				4	
			2	8	7			
	1				5	3		
3					1			4
4	7					9		
		2	7		4		5	

6			2	5	8			
	7				1			
	8					3	9	2
	5	9					6	
			8		4			
	3					4	1	
7	4	5					2	
			3				5	
			4	6	5			9

7			3					
	3				5	7		6
1	8			7				
	1	2						
5		4	6		8	3		9
						6	5	
				5			4	1
8		7	2				6	
					9			3

217

							2	9
		3						
		8	6		3	4		5
	3				9	7		1
1				7				2
9		7	5				3	
3		4	1		5	8		
						9		
6	1							

218

3	8			4	1			6
		9						4
			7			2		
	7	5						2
9		2		6		4		1
8						7	5	
		1			9			
6						1		
7			1	5			2	3

219

9			8			5	6	
					9		3	2
7				1	3			4
							7	
4		6				1		3
	7							
8			4	5				7
2	9		3					
	5	7			1			6

220

5			1					9
	7		4		3	5		
					2		8	
		8					2	5
1		7				6		4
6	2					3		
	1		2					
		3	8		5		1	
7					6			3

114

221

				2		7		6
						5	2	4
			6			9		
7	8				9	4		2
	4			7			3	
1		9	2				6	7
		4			8			
9	3	8						
6		1		4				

222

	8				6			2
2		5		3	4		6	8
	4					3		
7								
	1		2		5		7	
								9
		1					8	
5	7		3	6		9		1
6			7				4	

				4				
7								9
	9		5	3		6	7	2
	3					2	4	1
				7				
4	5	8					9	
2	4	5		8	6		1	
9								7
				9				

		7	6					4
						3	7	6
		1			4			9
8				4			3	
			8	5	3			
	4			9				7
3			7			2		
9	8	2						
5					1	6		

225

			2	3				
	9		8					1
	3	7			6		8	2
		5	9				2	
4								9
	2				3	4		
5	6		1			8	9	
2					5		6	
				6	9			

226

	1	5		6				
			1	9		3	2	
					3	6		
2						4	5	
		1		5		7		
	3	4						1
		3	9					
	6	8		1	4			
				2		9	8	

227

	9			7	2			
		4	8	9			2	
			5		4			9
8						1	4	
	7			6			9	
	3	2						8
5			6		1			
	4			5	9	3		
			7	4			1	

228

	9	3	6		2	5		
		7						
6	4				8	1		
3							1	
	5			1			9	
	7							4
		6	5				4	7
						3		
		5	3		4	9	2	

229

4		1		6				
		9	8				1	2
	5		4			7		6
			1			5		
	8			9			4	
		3			4			
8		7			5		9	
6	1				3	2		
				7		3		8

230

7						8		5
	9				8			
	5			1	7			
6							5	1
		5	3	7	1	6		
8	2							3
			9	5			3	
			1				8	
2		3						4

9	7	2					5	
			2				9	
		5	4			8		
2				7			8	3
	1						2	
8	5			6				7
		7			3	1		
	8				4			
	4					6	3	8

3				7	8			
2	6		1	4				
		1	9				5	
6		9						
8	5			6			1	9
						4		3
	2				6	5		
				8	1		7	2
			4	3				1

						9	6	
9	6			4	7		3	
8	5							
1	7	4		8				
				9				
				7		3	4	1
							5	6
	3		8	2			1	7
	4	8						

	4	7	1				2	
	8				7	6		
							5	4
		9		7			1	
			3	4	9			
	5			6		8		
2	9							
		4	5				7	
	7				8	4	3	

8	5	2			4			
6			3				5	2
1		3					6	8
	9			5			7	
4	6					3		9
5	4				8			3
			9			6	1	4

						5		
		9		7		2		
		7	1	9				3
1	9		6					
	2	8		3		7	5	
					8		6	4
7				4	5	9		
		1		8		3		
		3						

					6		4	
3			1	9				
8		4						5
6	7		2		5			
9	8						7	4
			9		7		2	1
5						3		7
				2	1			6
	9		3					

4						7		
9					6		5	
6			7		8		4	2
						8	1	5
		6		1		2		
7	1	3						
3	7		4		1			8
	4		6					1
		2						9

7	1			3	4		9	
5		9					2	
8				5			7	
				6	3			
		6				5		
			5	9				
	5			2				7
	3					8		6
	7		3	4			5	1

				3				1
	8	6		9			5	7
2	5							
	3		4			1		
		8	9		6	5		
		2			1		4	
							6	3
6	9			5		2	1	
4				1				

	3				1	6		
6	4					7		
			6		9			3
4			9	1				5
	9			6			1	
7				5	3			8
2			8		6			
		6					9	4
		5	1				8	

5		9	7		4			
	3					5		
6						2		
	9		2		5	3		
	2	4		6		9	5	
		5	9		1		8	
		7						5
		1					2	
			5		2	1		8

243

	7							3
				5			2	
8	3			2				9
		4			7		5	
3	8		6		5		1	2
	2		1			3		
6				1			7	8
	9			4				
1							6	

244

		1		2		3	6	
	6					1	5	
	2		1					9
					7			
7		2	9		6	4		8
			3					
8					5		9	
	5	9					3	
	1	4		7		6		

7				1				5
	9		4	2		3		1
					5			
		8				9	6	
		6	8	7	9	1		
	3	2				5		
			7					
4		9		5	6		1	
8				4				9

			2			4		
	7	9	5		3			
	5	4					2	9
4	8				2			5
1			7				8	4
6	2					8	9	
			9		1	7	6	
		3			7			

Puzzle 247

	6				9	4		
		7	1					
	8			4		2	9	
2			6	5				3
		8		3		9		
6				8	7			4
	3	4		6			5	
					3	6		
		6	2				3	

Puzzle 248

	8							
5		7	8				2	1
2	9				1	3		
						6	7	
6			9	4	5			3
	3	9						
		4	1				3	8
8	1				6	4		2
							5	

	8	5						2
		7		6				
	4			9			6	3
		4		1				6
8			6		9			4
1				2		9		
3	1			7			4	
				5		1		
4						3	2	

	2					6	1	5
6	5	1			2			8
				4		9		3
			6	9	7			
8		7		5				
2			3			5	4	1
1	8	6					2	

			3	8	2	9		
6					9		8	3
						7		5
	4				7			2
3				2				6
1			6				9	
4		8						
2	3		8					7
		1	5	7	3			

	4				2	5		1
		3				7		
	8			7			3	
	6	2		5	4		7	
				8				
	9		6	3		1	2	
	2			1			9	
		9				6		
3		1	9				5	

4		1	2					3
				3				
	9	6	5	8				
7				9			4	1
		9				8		
8	6			7				5
				2	4	5	1	
				5				
2					3	9		7

	8						7	2
9	4			5				
5					1		3	
				8	1			6
	6		7		2		5	
3		2	5					
	7		9					3
				7			8	5
6	1						9	

255

		7				2	5	
6			7	8				
				9	5			
5	4	6		3			1	
2				6				8
	9			2		6	4	3
			4	7				
			5	3				9
	5	4				7		

256

			8		1		4	
5		4				9	8	2
		6						
		3	7					8
2	4			1			7	3
1					6	2		
						7		
8	3	9				5		4
	5		6		4			

Puzzle 257

		2						6
	3			9		5		2
		7			3	8	4	
	4	8				6		
5				8				3
		3				4	8	
	2	4	6			7		
7		6		4			9	
8						2		

Puzzle 258

	9			1	8		4	
			2		4	3		
1			7				8	
7			3					
	6			9			2	
					7			9
	2				3			5
		3	4		1			
	7		9	8			3	

	5	1				8		
	7		3	1			6	
6				4		5		
							3	9
8		9				7		4
2	3							
		5		6				8
	6			8	7		9	
		4				6	1	

					3	1	2	5
		7				8	9	
				8	2	3		
	4				7			
6			5		4			7
			2				4	
		2	8	3				
	5	6				7		
3	8	9	1					

		2			1		3	8
3								
	6			4				5
5			2	1		7	8	
			4		6			
	7	9		8	5			2
1				5			6	
								3
6	2		7			9		

	1		8	2	7			
	8	7						
						7		3
7	5				6		2	
		2	9	3	5	4		
	4		7				9	6
1		5						
						8	6	
			2	5	3		7	

Puzzle 263

1						8	2	3
3							9	
8	9		7	5		6		
			3		2			
				8				
			5		7			
		6		1	9		8	2
	8							5
2	7	1						6

Puzzle 264

9					7			
							4	
1	3		5	2		9		6
7		4					5	1
	9			5			6	
6	5					3		4
4		5		9	1		3	2
	6							
			3					7

	2				3	9		
			2	7		5	8	
					8		4	3
	1		4		5			
6								2
			1		9		5	
4	6		3					
	5	1		9	2			
		9	7				6	

		3	7		6			
6	8					2		
1								7
9				6	7			5
		1		8		6		
8			2	1				9
7								2
		2					5	1
			9		4	7		

	2		4		3			6
				1				
	9			8			4	
	3	5	1		7	8		
1								3
		6	3		9	1	5	
	6			4			2	
				7				
9			2		1		8	

				6		9		
4			8	9		2		
8					5	7		
	7	5						4
	3			4			2	
9						3	6	
		9	5					3
		8		3	1			9
		6		8				

	7	8		2	1			
2	1		5					
4					3	6		
	5			1		4	6	
	6	2		5			7	
		7	8					6
					7		9	5
			4	6		1	3	

5			3					4
3			5		7			
	9		8				6	
	1			3		8		5
			4	2	8			
8		9		1			2	
	6				3		5	
			2		4			9
1					6			7

271

				2				9
	7		4	5			6	3
		4			7			
	6							2
7			9	3	6			8
8							5	
			1			2		
9	4			8	5		1	
3				7				

272

		6	3					9
				7				
		3		4	1	5		7
	3						7	1
	1	5				3	9	
8	2						6	
3		9	7	6		8		
				1				
4					3	7		

	7							5
4							6	9
		6	8			7	3	
7	3		9	8	2			
			3	7	6		9	2
	4	2				3	1	
9	8							3
6							2	

				4			3	
7	5			2			8	9
		1			5			
		9			2	4		
4			3	1	7			5
		2	5			7		
			7			9		
9	2			3			7	1
	8			5				

2 7 5

3		2			9			7
4				6	1	9		
			8					
	3	4					2	6
	1			8			7	
7	5					1	4	
					7			
		1	6	3				2
6			1			4		3

2 7 6

8			5	2				
9		6				1		
	3	2	1					8
2								9
6	8			5			7	3
3								5
7					8	5	4	
		3				2		7
				7	4			1

Puzzle 277

	9				2	4	7	
		1		9			8	
			8		7			
	4						2	8
7	3			8			4	9
9	6						1	
			2		3			
	2			5		9		
	1	4	6				3	

Puzzle 278

4		5			3			
1	9							
	8	3	2			4		
	6		4				3	
	5	1		3		6	9	
	7				9		1	
		7			2	1	4	
							7	8
			7			5		3

4					3	6		7
2	7	9	6					
1				4			8	
5					4			
	4						9	
			8					1
	1			9				5
					8	3	2	9
9		5	7					6

				5	1		6	
			7			3	5	8
			9			1		2
				2				9
6		8				5		4
3				8				
5		9			6			
8	6	4			7			
	3		8	4				

7		1						
	5	4	2		8		7	9
	8			5				
1		5	8					
		3		6		4		
					4	1		5
				4			3	
4	2		1		6	5	8	
						2		1

9		5	3		4		6	
							4	
4		6			5	2		
	9	1	7					
		3				4		
					8	3	1	
		7	2			6		3
	6							
	1		4		9	7		8

Puzzle 283

3				8				
								5
	7		5			9	2	1
7		2	4		8	5		
9								6
		4	6		7	3		2
8	1	9			4		6	
2								
				2				4

Puzzle 284

1	2						3	
6		5	8	7	4			
		7						4
5					6		9	
			7		2			
	8		3					2
2						3		
			5	1	9	2		8
	6						1	5

		2	4					
4				3	2			
			8		7		4	6
		4				1	2	
	1		7	9	8		6	
	5	6				3		
5	7		3		1			
			5	8				4
					9	8		

	1	2	3			6	7	
					7	1		5
5			2					
9	2		6					3
				4				
4					9		6	1
					2			9
3		9	5					
	8	1			4	7	5	

	1	5	2					4
8								
		3	5			2	9	
		6		3				2
	8		6	1	4		7	
5				2		6		
	5	1			9	7		
								3
9					2	5	6	

		8	4			5		
	3		8		7		1	2
7								9
				2			4	
			3	9	1			
	6			7				
5								4
2	9		1		6		5	
		4			2	7		

			9		2		4	3
8					5		7	
				7	1		2	8
3						7		
		2		4		6		
		5						1
1	3		8	6				
	6		3					9
2	9		1		4			

4			6			9		
		9		4		8		
		6		3		1	4	
			9	8			3	
		3		1		2		
	9			2	5			
	2	1		9		6		
		8		7		5		
		5			4			8

						8		3
7		2	8					
				1	6	7		
4					5	9		
1		6	4	9	2	5		8
		8	3					4
		3	9	6				
					3	4		5
2		4						

5						7	2	
			1	4	5	9		
		9	8					
3	5				4			
		7		9		8		
			3				6	4
					6	3		
		5	7	8	3			
	9	3						8

	5		1		4			2
8			7				3	9
	3	2						
5		7						
	6		4		2		1	
						3		6
						8	5	
3	4				1			7
2			3		5		4	

	5	2			8			4
	7			6				
8					7		6	
5	8			4	2			
	6						8	
			6	8			1	3
	2		7					1
				1			9	
4			8			2	5	

9					5			4
	5	4	2	6		9		
	7	2					5	
			6	7				
6				1				8
				8	3			
	2					8	4	
		8		4	7	1	2	
1			9					7

2				5		7		
		1			6	8		5
			7		4			
					9	2		4
5			8		1			9
9		8	6					
			4		8			
6		3	9			5		
		7		1				2

9						3		5
	1						6	
2	8	6		3	1			
			1	6			2	
		1		2		7		
	4			7	8			
			6	1		4	5	3
	5						8	
4		7						1

		4						
3	1			8			5	9
5			9					
	6		3	5			8	
4				1				2
	8			2	9		1	
					2			6
1	5			7			2	4
						5		

9	2		3		8			
				4	6			
5			7			3		
			5		7		3	
8		2				5		7
	5		9		3			
		7			6			2
		8	1					
			8		2		7	6

1					8		6	
			9			1		
	6		1	5		9		2
			8		9		7	
		8				3		
	1		4		7			
6		9		1	5		8	
		4			2			
	3		7					5

1

1	2	6	7	5	9	3	4	8
4	7	5	1	3	8	2	9	6
8	3	9	4	2	6	5	1	7
3	5	4	8	7	1	9	6	2
9	1	8	2	6	5	4	7	3
7	6	2	9	4	3	1	8	5
6	8	3	5	1	4	7	2	9
2	9	1	3	8	7	6	5	4
5	4	7	6	9	2	8	3	1

2

2	5	4	7	9	8	6	1	3
9	3	6	1	2	5	4	7	8
1	8	7	6	4	3	2	9	5
7	6	3	4	8	1	9	5	2
8	2	1	5	6	9	3	4	7
5	4	9	3	7	2	1	8	6
3	9	5	2	1	7	8	6	4
4	1	2	8	5	6	7	3	9
6	7	8	9	3	4	5	2	1

3

5	4	7	2	3	9	8	6	1
3	8	2	1	6	5	9	7	4
6	9	1	7	4	8	5	3	2
7	5	8	6	1	4	3	2	9
9	6	4	3	5	2	7	1	8
1	2	3	9	8	7	6	4	5
2	3	6	8	9	1	4	5	7
8	7	5	4	2	6	1	9	3
4	1	9	5	7	3	2	8	6

4

4	1	6	3	2	8	7	5	9
8	3	7	9	5	1	4	6	2
5	9	2	7	6	4	8	3	1
1	6	4	5	8	3	9	2	7
2	5	9	4	1	7	6	8	3
7	8	3	6	9	2	1	4	5
9	4	1	2	3	6	5	7	8
3	7	5	8	4	9	2	1	6
6	2	8	1	7	5	3	9	4

5

3	5	8	6	1	4	7	2	9
9	4	6	5	2	7	3	8	1
1	7	2	8	3	9	5	6	4
8	6	5	9	4	3	2	1	7
4	2	9	7	5	1	6	3	8
7	3	1	2	6	8	9	4	5
2	1	7	4	9	6	8	5	3
6	9	3	1	8	5	4	7	2
5	8	4	3	7	2	1	9	6

6

5	3	4	2	8	6	1	7	9
7	8	1	4	9	3	5	6	2
6	9	2	7	1	5	3	8	4
1	5	7	8	6	4	9	2	3
2	4	9	3	7	1	8	5	6
3	6	8	9	5	2	4	1	7
4	1	6	5	2	9	7	3	8
8	2	3	1	4	7	6	9	5
9	7	5	6	3	8	2	4	1

7

9	4	3	1	8	6	2	7	5
1	7	8	5	2	3	4	9	6
5	6	2	4	9	7	1	3	8
4	5	1	2	6	9	3	8	7
7	2	6	3	4	8	5	1	9
3	8	9	7	1	5	6	2	4
2	3	5	8	7	4	9	6	1
8	9	4	6	3	1	7	5	2
6	1	7	9	5	2	8	4	3

8

2	7	4	5	6	3	1	9	8
8	3	1	9	7	2	4	5	6
5	9	6	8	4	1	3	2	7
9	4	8	2	1	7	6	3	5
3	5	7	6	9	8	2	4	1
1	6	2	4	3	5	8	7	9
4	2	5	1	8	9	7	6	3
7	1	9	3	2	6	5	8	4
6	8	3	7	5	4	9	1	2

9

8	3	4	1	9	5	7	2	6
7	9	6	4	3	2	8	5	1
5	2	1	8	7	6	4	9	3
2	4	3	7	8	1	9	6	5
1	8	5	3	6	9	2	7	4
9	6	7	5	2	4	3	1	8
6	5	2	9	4	3	1	8	7
4	1	8	2	5	7	6	3	9
3	7	9	6	1	8	5	4	2

10

1	6	9	3	7	8	4	2	5
3	7	5	2	4	9	8	6	1
8	2	4	1	5	6	9	7	3
4	8	1	7	2	3	5	9	6
7	9	6	5	8	1	2	3	4
5	3	2	9	6	4	7	1	8
2	4	3	8	1	7	6	5	9
9	5	8	6	3	2	1	4	7
6	1	7	4	9	5	3	8	2

11

3	6	5	4	1	7	9	2	8
7	4	2	3	8	9	6	5	1
1	9	8	2	6	5	4	3	7
9	2	1	8	3	6	5	7	4
8	7	3	5	2	4	1	6	9
4	5	6	7	9	1	2	8	3
6	8	4	9	7	2	3	1	5
5	1	7	6	4	3	8	9	2
2	3	9	1	5	8	7	4	6

12

2	5	4	3	8	7	9	6	1
8	7	6	9	1	5	2	3	4
3	1	9	2	4	6	8	7	5
4	6	2	1	7	8	3	5	9
5	9	8	6	3	4	7	1	2
1	3	7	5	9	2	4	8	6
9	8	5	7	2	1	6	4	3
6	4	3	8	5	9	1	2	7
7	2	1	4	6	3	5	9	8

13

8	5	6	3	1	7	9	2	4
3	2	4	9	8	5	7	1	6
9	7	1	2	6	4	3	5	8
1	6	5	4	7	2	8	3	9
2	3	7	8	9	1	4	6	5
4	9	8	5	3	6	1	7	2
5	8	2	7	4	3	6	9	1
6	4	3	1	5	9	2	8	7
7	1	9	6	2	8	5	4	3

14

2	6	3	9	4	5	7	1	8
8	9	1	7	3	6	2	5	4
4	5	7	1	8	2	6	9	3
1	7	4	2	6	8	9	3	5
9	3	6	5	1	7	8	4	2
5	8	2	3	9	4	1	6	7
7	2	9	4	5	1	3	8	6
6	1	5	8	2	3	4	7	9
3	4	8	6	7	9	5	2	1

15

8	4	7	3	5	6	1	2	9
6	5	3	9	2	1	4	7	8
9	2	1	7	4	8	5	3	6
2	8	6	4	1	3	9	5	7
4	7	9	5	6	2	3	8	1
1	3	5	8	9	7	2	6	4
7	9	4	2	8	5	6	1	3
3	6	2	1	7	9	8	4	5
5	1	8	6	3	4	7	9	2

16

5	9	8	6	7	3	2	1	4
3	2	4	5	1	8	6	7	9
1	7	6	9	4	2	5	8	3
7	6	9	8	5	4	3	2	1
2	3	1	7	6	9	4	5	8
4	8	5	2	3	1	7	9	6
8	4	2	3	9	5	1	6	7
9	1	7	4	2	6	8	3	5
6	5	3	1	8	7	9	4	2

17

1	5	9	3	8	2	7	4	6
7	2	8	4	1	6	9	3	5
3	4	6	7	5	9	2	8	1
6	1	3	8	9	4	5	2	7
9	7	4	2	3	5	6	1	8
2	8	5	1	6	7	3	9	4
5	6	1	9	4	3	8	7	2
4	9	7	6	2	8	1	5	3
8	3	2	5	7	1	4	6	9

18

1	5	2	6	7	9	3	4	8
6	7	9	4	8	3	5	1	2
4	8	3	2	5	1	9	7	6
7	6	5	9	4	2	1	8	3
9	3	8	7	1	6	2	5	4
2	4	1	5	3	8	6	9	7
5	9	6	8	2	4	7	3	1
8	1	7	3	6	5	4	2	9
3	2	4	1	9	7	8	6	5

19

7	6	3	9	2	1	4	5	8
5	2	1	6	4	8	7	9	3
9	4	8	5	7	3	6	1	2
3	7	2	1	9	4	8	6	5
6	1	9	2	8	5	3	4	7
4	8	5	7	3	6	1	2	9
1	3	7	4	5	2	9	8	6
2	9	4	8	6	7	5	3	1
8	5	6	3	1	9	2	7	4

20

1	8	9	6	5	2	3	4	7
5	4	2	1	7	3	9	6	8
7	3	6	4	8	9	2	1	5
4	9	1	8	6	5	7	3	2
2	6	5	9	3	7	4	8	1
8	7	3	2	1	4	5	9	6
9	1	7	5	4	8	6	2	3
3	2	8	7	9	6	1	5	4
6	5	4	3	2	1	8	7	9

21

8	1	7	5	4	3	2	9	6
5	6	3	9	2	7	1	4	8
4	2	9	8	6	1	7	5	3
3	8	2	4	7	9	6	1	5
6	9	1	3	5	2	4	8	7
7	5	4	1	8	6	3	2	9
1	7	8	2	3	5	9	6	4
9	4	6	7	1	8	5	3	2
2	3	5	6	9	4	8	7	1

22

3	6	1	2	8	5	7	4	9
4	7	9	1	6	3	2	5	8
2	8	5	7	9	4	6	1	3
7	9	3	4	5	8	1	2	6
6	1	4	3	7	2	9	8	5
5	2	8	9	1	6	3	7	4
9	4	7	8	3	1	5	6	2
8	3	6	5	2	7	4	9	1
1	5	2	6	4	9	8	3	7

23

1	8	7	4	2	5	6	3	9
9	4	5	1	3	6	8	2	7
3	2	6	7	8	9	1	5	4
7	9	2	5	1	3	4	8	6
5	6	3	8	7	4	2	9	1
4	1	8	9	6	2	3	7	5
2	7	4	3	5	1	9	6	8
8	3	1	6	9	7	5	4	2
6	5	9	2	4	8	7	1	3

24

9	7	1	6	3	4	8	5	2
6	5	4	1	2	8	7	3	9
3	2	8	5	7	9	1	6	4
5	6	9	8	1	7	4	2	3
1	4	7	3	5	2	9	8	6
2	8	3	9	4	6	5	1	7
4	9	5	2	6	1	3	7	8
8	1	6	7	9	3	2	4	5
7	3	2	4	8	5	6	9	1

25

1	6	5	7	8	2	3	4	9
8	7	4	6	9	3	5	1	2
2	3	9	5	1	4	7	6	8
6	5	1	3	4	8	2	9	7
4	9	7	2	6	5	8	3	1
3	2	8	1	7	9	4	5	6
7	1	3	4	2	6	9	8	5
9	4	6	8	5	7	1	2	3
5	8	2	9	3	1	6	7	4

26

8	7	5	4	9	2	6	1	3
3	6	1	8	7	5	9	4	2
9	2	4	6	3	1	5	7	8
6	4	2	9	8	3	7	5	1
7	1	3	2	5	6	4	8	9
5	9	8	1	4	7	2	3	6
2	5	7	3	1	9	8	6	4
1	8	6	7	2	4	3	9	5
4	3	9	5	6	8	1	2	7

27

7	6	5	3	9	1	8	2	4
8	4	2	6	7	5	3	1	9
3	1	9	2	4	8	5	7	6
1	8	7	4	5	9	2	6	3
6	9	4	7	3	2	1	8	5
2	5	3	1	8	6	4	9	7
5	7	8	9	1	4	6	3	2
4	3	6	8	2	7	9	5	1
9	2	1	5	6	3	7	4	8

28

8	2	4	5	3	1	9	6	7
1	7	9	4	2	6	5	3	8
5	3	6	8	9	7	1	4	2
9	8	1	6	7	3	2	5	4
2	5	7	1	8	4	6	9	3
4	6	3	9	5	2	8	7	1
3	9	2	7	6	8	4	1	5
7	4	5	2	1	9	3	8	6
6	1	8	3	4	5	7	2	9

29

2	8	1	9	5	6	4	7	3
6	3	5	7	4	2	1	8	9
9	4	7	1	8	3	2	6	5
1	6	2	8	7	9	3	5	4
4	9	3	2	6	5	8	1	7
5	7	8	4	3	1	6	9	2
7	1	9	6	2	4	5	3	8
3	2	6	5	9	8	7	4	1
8	5	4	3	1	7	9	2	6

30

8	4	9	2	7	3	6	5	1
6	2	3	5	1	8	9	7	4
7	1	5	9	4	6	2	8	3
5	7	6	3	9	4	8	1	2
9	8	4	6	2	1	7	3	5
2	3	1	7	8	5	4	6	9
4	5	2	8	3	7	1	9	6
1	6	8	4	5	9	3	2	7
3	9	7	1	6	2	5	4	8

31

3	2	8	1	6	7	5	4	9
9	5	1	2	4	3	7	6	8
4	7	6	8	5	9	2	1	3
1	6	9	4	8	2	3	5	7
5	3	2	9	7	1	6	8	4
7	8	4	6	3	5	1	9	2
2	4	5	3	9	6	8	7	1
6	9	3	7	1	8	4	2	5
8	1	7	5	2	4	9	3	6

32

4	7	5	2	6	3	1	9	8
1	9	6	7	8	4	3	5	2
3	2	8	5	9	1	7	6	4
2	4	3	6	7	5	8	1	9
5	6	9	3	1	8	4	2	7
7	8	1	4	2	9	5	3	6
9	3	2	8	5	7	6	4	1
8	1	4	9	3	6	2	7	5
6	5	7	1	4	2	9	8	3

33

9	3	8	4	6	5	2	7	1
4	2	7	8	3	1	5	6	9
1	6	5	7	9	2	8	3	4
6	5	4	3	1	8	9	2	7
8	7	3	9	2	4	6	1	5
2	1	9	6	5	7	4	8	3
3	4	2	5	7	6	1	9	8
5	9	6	1	8	3	7	4	2
7	8	1	2	4	9	3	5	6

34

5	1	2	3	4	7	8	9	6
4	3	6	1	9	8	5	2	7
9	7	8	5	2	6	1	3	4
6	9	1	8	3	4	2	7	5
3	4	5	2	7	1	9	6	8
8	2	7	6	5	9	4	1	3
2	5	9	7	8	3	6	4	1
7	6	4	9	1	5	3	8	2
1	8	3	4	6	2	7	5	9

35

2	1	7	6	4	9	8	3	5
8	6	5	1	7	3	9	4	2
9	4	3	5	8	2	7	1	6
4	8	1	2	6	5	3	9	7
5	7	9	4	3	1	2	6	8
3	2	6	8	9	7	1	5	4
6	9	4	7	1	8	5	2	3
1	5	8	3	2	4	6	7	9
7	3	2	9	5	6	4	8	1

36

4	6	5	9	1	8	2	7	3
3	1	9	7	4	2	5	8	6
2	8	7	5	3	6	9	4	1
5	4	6	8	2	1	3	9	7
8	7	1	3	6	9	4	2	5
9	3	2	4	7	5	1	6	8
1	5	8	2	9	7	6	3	4
6	2	3	1	8	4	7	5	9
7	9	4	6	5	3	8	1	2

37

9	2	5	3	8	7	1	4	6
4	6	1	9	5	2	8	7	3
3	7	8	4	6	1	5	2	9
8	9	7	5	3	4	6	1	2
6	3	4	1	2	8	7	9	5
1	5	2	7	9	6	4	3	8
7	8	9	6	1	3	2	5	4
2	1	3	8	4	5	9	6	7
5	4	6	2	7	9	3	8	1

38

9	3	8	7	4	5	1	2	6
2	6	7	8	3	1	9	4	5
4	5	1	2	9	6	3	7	8
1	8	5	4	7	3	2	6	9
6	2	3	9	1	8	7	5	4
7	4	9	5	6	2	8	3	1
3	7	6	1	8	4	5	9	2
8	9	2	6	5	7	4	1	3
5	1	4	3	2	9	6	8	7

39

8	4	2	6	3	5	7	1	9
6	9	1	8	7	2	4	5	3
3	7	5	9	1	4	6	2	8
2	1	4	3	6	7	8	9	5
5	3	8	1	4	9	2	7	6
7	6	9	2	5	8	1	3	4
4	2	6	5	9	1	3	8	7
9	8	3	7	2	6	5	4	1
1	5	7	4	8	3	9	6	2

40

7	1	9	2	3	6	4	5	8
2	6	3	5	4	8	9	1	7
4	8	5	7	9	1	2	3	6
6	9	7	8	5	2	3	4	1
5	3	2	6	1	4	8	7	9
8	4	1	9	7	3	5	6	2
3	2	8	4	6	7	1	9	5
9	7	4	1	8	5	6	2	3
1	5	6	3	2	9	7	8	4

4/1

3	4	8	9	7	2	1	5	6
1	6	5	4	8	3	2	9	7
2	9	7	1	6	5	3	4	8
8	2	1	3	4	9	6	7	5
9	3	6	7	5	8	4	1	2
5	7	4	2	1	6	9	8	3
6	8	9	5	2	4	7	3	1
4	1	2	8	3	7	5	6	9
7	5	3	6	9	1	8	2	4

4/2

9	4	6	1	3	5	7	2	8
7	8	3	9	2	6	5	1	4
2	1	5	7	8	4	9	6	3
1	9	2	4	6	8	3	5	7
3	7	8	5	1	9	6	4	2
6	5	4	3	7	2	8	9	1
8	3	9	2	5	1	4	7	6
5	2	7	6	4	3	1	8	9
4	6	1	8	9	7	2	3	5

4/3

7	1	6	5	2	8	4	3	9
3	5	9	1	4	6	2	8	7
4	2	8	3	7	9	5	6	1
9	6	5	2	8	1	3	7	4
2	3	4	9	6	7	1	5	8
8	7	1	4	3	5	9	2	6
6	4	3	8	1	2	7	9	5
1	9	7	6	5	3	8	4	2
5	8	2	7	9	4	6	1	3

4/4

6	9	4	8	5	2	7	3	1
8	1	7	6	9	3	2	5	4
5	2	3	1	4	7	6	8	9
2	7	6	9	8	1	5	4	3
4	3	1	7	2	5	9	6	8
9	5	8	4	3	6	1	2	7
3	8	5	2	1	9	4	7	6
1	6	2	3	7	4	8	9	5
7	4	9	5	6	8	3	1	2

4/5

3	2	8	1	7	4	5	9	6
5	6	4	9	8	2	7	1	3
9	7	1	3	6	5	8	2	4
2	5	6	8	1	9	3	4	7
8	4	9	7	5	3	1	6	2
7	1	3	4	2	6	9	5	8
4	3	2	5	9	8	6	7	1
6	9	7	2	3	1	4	8	5
1	8	5	6	4	7	2	3	9

4/6

3	2	9	4	6	8	5	1	7
5	6	1	9	3	7	8	2	4
8	7	4	5	2	1	9	6	3
1	5	6	7	8	4	2	3	9
2	4	7	1	9	3	6	8	5
9	8	3	6	5	2	7	4	1
4	9	5	8	1	6	3	7	2
7	3	8	2	4	5	1	9	6
6	1	2	3	7	9	4	5	8

4/7

5	7	9	2	6	4	1	8	3
6	3	1	5	8	9	2	4	7
8	4	2	3	7	1	5	6	9
2	9	6	1	5	8	7	3	4
4	1	8	7	2	3	9	5	6
7	5	3	4	9	6	8	1	2
1	2	5	6	3	7	4	9	8
9	6	4	8	1	2	3	7	5
3	8	7	9	4	5	6	2	1

4/8

2	5	1	4	6	3	8	7	9
8	9	7	5	1	2	3	4	6
3	4	6	7	8	9	2	1	5
9	7	3	2	4	8	6	5	1
6	8	4	3	5	1	7	9	2
5	1	2	9	7	6	4	8	3
1	3	8	6	9	7	5	2	4
7	2	5	1	3	4	9	6	8
4	6	9	8	2	5	1	3	7

49

8	4	3	1	7	2	5	6	9
1	7	9	6	3	5	2	4	8
2	5	6	8	4	9	3	7	1
6	9	7	5	2	3	1	8	4
3	1	5	4	8	7	9	2	6
4	2	8	9	6	1	7	3	5
5	8	2	7	9	4	6	1	3
7	6	1	3	5	8	4	9	2
9	3	4	2	1	6	8	5	7

50

3	6	1	4	8	9	2	7	5
5	7	8	1	2	3	9	6	4
2	9	4	6	5	7	1	3	8
6	5	2	9	7	4	3	8	1
8	4	9	3	1	5	7	2	6
1	3	7	8	6	2	5	4	9
4	2	6	5	3	1	8	9	7
9	1	3	7	4	8	6	5	2
7	8	5	2	9	6	4	1	3

51

2	4	8	5	6	7	9	3	1
9	5	1	8	2	3	4	7	6
6	7	3	9	1	4	5	2	8
3	1	4	6	7	9	8	5	2
8	6	5	3	4	2	1	9	7
7	9	2	1	5	8	3	6	4
1	8	9	7	3	6	2	4	5
5	2	6	4	9	1	7	8	3
4	3	7	2	8	5	6	1	9

52

2	9	7	6	4	1	3	8	5
5	4	6	9	3	8	1	7	2
1	8	3	2	7	5	6	9	4
9	7	2	8	6	3	4	5	1
8	6	5	4	1	7	9	2	3
3	1	4	5	2	9	8	6	7
6	3	9	7	5	4	2	1	8
4	5	8	1	9	2	7	3	6
7	2	1	3	8	6	5	4	9

53

1	9	6	7	2	8	5	3	4
3	7	8	5	1	4	2	6	9
5	4	2	9	6	3	8	7	1
6	8	9	1	7	2	3	4	5
7	5	1	3	4	6	9	2	8
2	3	4	8	5	9	7	1	6
9	6	7	2	8	1	4	5	3
8	1	5	4	3	7	6	9	2
4	2	3	6	9	5	1	8	7

54

7	5	6	8	3	9	2	4	1
4	1	8	2	5	6	7	3	9
9	3	2	7	1	4	8	5	6
3	9	4	1	8	7	6	2	5
2	7	1	6	9	5	3	8	4
6	8	5	3	4	2	9	1	7
1	2	7	5	6	3	4	9	8
8	6	9	4	2	1	5	7	3
5	4	3	9	7	8	1	6	2

55

2	8	3	7	5	1	6	9	4
7	5	4	9	3	6	1	2	8
6	9	1	4	2	8	5	7	3
4	1	7	2	9	3	8	5	6
8	6	5	1	4	7	2	3	9
3	2	9	6	8	5	7	4	1
9	3	6	8	7	2	4	1	5
1	4	2	5	6	9	3	8	7
5	7	8	3	1	4	9	6	2

56

7	3	6	8	5	1	2	9	4
8	1	5	9	4	2	3	7	6
4	2	9	7	3	6	5	1	8
3	4	1	6	8	5	7	2	9
6	8	2	3	7	9	1	4	5
9	5	7	1	2	4	6	8	3
5	7	3	4	1	8	9	6	2
1	6	8	2	9	3	4	5	7
2	9	4	5	6	7	8	3	1

57

7	8	5	4	9	3	1	6	2
9	6	2	1	8	7	5	4	3
3	1	4	2	5	6	7	8	9
8	9	1	6	7	5	3	2	4
4	3	7	8	1	2	9	5	6
5	2	6	3	4	9	8	1	7
2	4	9	5	3	1	6	7	8
6	5	3	7	2	8	4	9	1
1	7	8	9	6	4	2	3	5

58

7	1	2	8	9	5	4	3	6
8	3	6	7	2	4	5	1	9
5	4	9	1	3	6	8	2	7
2	5	7	3	6	8	9	4	1
3	8	1	9	4	7	6	5	2
6	9	4	5	1	2	7	8	3
1	6	5	4	7	3	2	9	8
9	2	8	6	5	1	3	7	4
4	7	3	2	8	9	1	6	5

59

3	8	7	4	5	9	1	2	6
1	2	9	3	6	8	7	5	4
4	6	5	7	2	1	3	9	8
8	5	6	1	9	7	2	4	3
7	4	2	5	3	6	9	8	1
9	3	1	8	4	2	5	6	7
5	1	8	2	7	4	6	3	9
2	9	4	6	1	3	8	7	5
6	7	3	9	8	5	4	1	2

60

4	1	5	3	2	7	9	6	8
8	6	9	1	5	4	3	2	7
7	3	2	8	6	9	5	4	1
9	5	8	7	4	6	1	3	2
6	2	1	5	3	8	7	9	4
3	7	4	9	1	2	8	5	6
5	9	6	4	7	1	2	8	3
2	8	7	6	9	3	4	1	5
1	4	3	2	8	5	6	7	9

61

8	6	2	4	7	9	1	5	3
7	1	5	8	2	3	6	4	9
4	3	9	1	5	6	7	2	8
2	9	1	6	3	4	8	7	5
3	8	6	7	9	5	4	1	2
5	7	4	2	8	1	3	9	6
9	4	7	5	6	8	2	3	1
6	2	3	9	1	7	5	8	4
1	5	8	3	4	2	9	6	7

62

6	9	8	4	3	5	1	2	7
3	2	5	1	6	7	4	8	9
4	7	1	2	8	9	6	3	5
5	8	6	7	4	1	3	9	2
7	1	4	3	9	2	8	5	6
2	3	9	6	5	8	7	1	4
8	6	2	9	1	4	5	7	3
9	5	3	8	7	6	2	4	1
1	4	7	5	2	3	9	6	8

63

7	3	4	1	2	9	6	8	5
1	2	8	7	5	6	3	9	4
6	5	9	8	4	3	7	1	2
9	7	2	5	1	4	8	6	3
3	6	5	2	9	8	4	7	1
8	4	1	3	6	7	5	2	9
4	1	7	9	8	5	2	3	6
2	8	6	4	3	1	9	5	7
5	9	3	6	7	2	1	4	8

64

2	7	6	9	1	3	8	5	4
8	4	3	6	7	5	9	1	2
9	5	1	4	8	2	6	7	3
7	2	9	1	3	8	4	6	5
1	3	4	7	5	6	2	9	8
5	6	8	2	9	4	1	3	7
6	1	2	3	4	7	5	8	9
4	8	7	5	6	9	3	2	1
3	9	5	8	2	1	7	4	6

6/5

6	1	3	4	7	5	9	2	8
9	8	5	6	3	2	7	4	1
4	2	7	8	9	1	6	5	3
2	5	8	7	1	4	3	6	9
7	3	6	2	5	9	1	8	4
1	9	4	3	8	6	5	7	2
8	4	9	1	6	7	2	3	5
3	7	1	5	2	8	4	9	6
5	6	2	9	4	3	8	1	7

6/6

7	6	8	2	5	3	9	1	4
4	5	3	9	7	1	2	6	8
1	2	9	4	6	8	7	3	5
6	3	4	8	2	7	5	9	1
5	8	1	3	9	6	4	2	7
2	9	7	5	1	4	6	8	3
3	1	5	6	4	9	8	7	2
8	4	6	7	3	2	1	5	9
9	7	2	1	8	5	3	4	6

6/7

7	3	4	1	9	2	5	6	8
9	1	5	8	4	6	2	7	3
6	2	8	3	5	7	4	1	9
3	5	2	6	1	4	8	9	7
1	4	6	7	8	9	3	2	5
8	9	7	2	3	5	6	4	1
4	6	3	9	7	8	1	5	2
2	7	1	5	6	3	9	8	4
5	8	9	4	2	1	7	3	6

6/8

8	5	3	9	4	6	1	7	2
7	1	2	8	5	3	9	6	4
6	9	4	1	2	7	5	3	8
9	6	5	3	8	4	7	2	1
4	3	1	2	7	5	8	9	6
2	8	7	6	9	1	3	4	5
5	2	9	7	6	8	4	1	3
3	4	6	5	1	9	2	8	7
1	7	8	4	3	2	6	5	9

6/9

6	1	2	8	5	9	4	3	7
3	8	4	7	2	6	9	5	1
7	9	5	3	4	1	2	6	8
5	4	8	1	3	7	6	2	9
9	3	7	6	8	2	1	4	5
2	6	1	5	9	4	7	8	3
1	2	3	4	7	8	5	9	6
8	7	9	2	6	5	3	1	4
4	5	6	9	1	3	8	7	2

7/0

5	2	8	9	4	3	6	1	7
1	9	7	5	2	6	4	8	3
3	4	6	8	7	1	2	9	5
6	5	1	2	8	4	3	7	9
4	7	9	1	3	5	8	2	6
2	8	3	6	9	7	1	5	4
9	3	2	7	6	8	5	4	1
8	1	4	3	5	9	7	6	2
7	6	5	4	1	2	9	3	8

7/1

7	2	4	5	1	6	9	3	8
8	1	6	4	9	3	5	7	2
3	9	5	7	2	8	6	4	1
9	6	3	8	4	2	1	5	7
4	7	1	9	6	5	2	8	3
2	5	8	1	3	7	4	9	6
5	3	2	6	7	4	8	1	9
6	8	9	3	5	1	7	2	4
1	4	7	2	8	9	3	6	5

7/2

4	2	5	7	6	3	8	9	1
7	3	8	2	1	9	5	6	4
1	9	6	8	4	5	2	3	7
5	1	4	6	7	2	9	8	3
6	8	9	5	3	1	4	7	2
3	7	2	4	9	8	6	1	5
2	5	1	9	8	7	3	4	6
9	6	7	3	5	4	1	2	8
8	4	3	1	2	6	7	5	9

73

1	7	9	4	2	6	8	5	3
3	8	5	7	9	1	4	6	2
6	2	4	8	5	3	9	7	1
5	1	2	9	7	4	3	8	6
9	3	7	6	8	2	1	4	5
8	4	6	1	3	5	2	9	7
2	6	8	3	4	7	5	1	9
4	5	1	2	6	9	7	3	8
7	9	3	5	1	8	6	2	4

74

3	2	7	9	8	5	4	6	1
4	9	8	3	1	6	2	7	5
5	6	1	2	4	7	8	9	3
2	5	6	8	7	1	9	3	4
9	7	3	5	2	4	6	1	8
1	8	4	6	9	3	5	2	7
8	3	5	7	6	9	1	4	2
6	4	2	1	3	8	7	5	9
7	1	9	4	5	2	3	8	6

75

7	3	4	2	9	5	1	6	8
9	1	2	8	6	7	3	5	4
5	6	8	1	4	3	9	7	2
2	8	6	9	1	4	7	3	5
3	9	5	7	8	2	4	1	6
1	4	7	5	3	6	2	8	9
6	5	9	3	2	1	8	4	7
8	7	3	4	5	9	6	2	1
4	2	1	6	7	8	5	9	3

76

3	6	8	9	5	1	7	4	2
2	7	4	8	6	3	5	1	9
9	5	1	7	4	2	8	3	6
1	8	3	6	2	5	9	7	4
7	2	9	4	1	8	3	6	5
5	4	6	3	9	7	2	8	1
8	9	5	1	3	6	4	2	7
4	1	7	2	8	9	6	5	3
6	3	2	5	7	4	1	9	8

77

5	7	8	3	2	9	6	4	1
2	1	9	5	4	6	8	3	7
6	3	4	8	1	7	5	9	2
7	4	2	6	3	1	9	8	5
8	5	1	9	7	4	2	6	3
9	6	3	2	8	5	7	1	4
3	9	7	1	5	8	4	2	6
1	8	5	4	6	2	3	7	9
4	2	6	7	9	3	1	5	8

78

4	8	3	9	6	7	5	1	2
1	9	2	8	5	3	4	7	6
5	6	7	1	2	4	3	9	8
6	3	5	2	1	9	8	4	7
2	7	8	6	4	5	9	3	1
9	1	4	3	7	8	2	6	5
7	4	6	5	9	2	1	8	3
3	5	9	7	8	1	6	2	4
8	2	1	4	3	6	7	5	9

79

2	5	7	6	4	3	1	8	9
4	8	3	1	5	9	2	7	6
1	9	6	7	2	8	4	5	3
9	6	1	8	3	5	7	4	2
5	7	2	4	6	1	9	3	8
3	4	8	2	9	7	5	6	1
8	2	5	3	1	4	6	9	7
7	1	4	9	8	6	3	2	5
6	3	9	5	7	2	8	1	4

80

5	8	2	3	1	9	7	6	4
6	3	7	4	2	8	5	9	1
9	1	4	7	6	5	8	3	2
4	6	5	9	7	1	2	8	3
7	9	1	2	8	3	6	4	5
3	2	8	5	4	6	9	1	7
1	7	6	8	5	4	3	2	9
8	5	3	1	9	2	4	7	6
2	4	9	6	3	7	1	5	8

8/1

5	9	3	1	7	2	4	6	8
4	1	6	8	9	3	7	5	2
8	2	7	6	5	4	9	3	1
7	3	2	4	1	6	5	8	9
6	8	5	7	2	9	3	1	4
1	4	9	3	8	5	2	7	6
9	7	1	2	3	8	6	4	5
2	6	8	5	4	7	1	9	3
3	5	4	9	6	1	8	2	7

8/2

3	9	1	2	5	8	4	6	7
6	8	4	3	1	7	2	5	9
5	7	2	6	9	4	3	8	1
9	2	8	5	7	3	6	1	4
4	3	5	1	2	6	7	9	8
7	1	6	4	8	9	5	2	3
8	6	9	7	3	2	1	4	5
1	4	3	8	6	5	9	7	2
2	5	7	9	4	1	8	3	6

8/3

6	2	8	5	4	9	7	3	1
9	1	7	8	3	6	5	2	4
3	4	5	2	7	1	8	9	6
4	9	2	7	8	3	1	6	5
7	6	3	1	2	5	9	4	8
8	5	1	6	9	4	3	7	2
1	3	9	4	5	2	6	8	7
5	8	4	9	6	7	2	1	3
2	7	6	3	1	8	4	5	9

8/4

2	6	8	1	7	4	3	5	9
1	5	4	2	9	3	7	6	8
7	3	9	5	6	8	2	4	1
6	4	7	3	2	1	8	9	5
3	2	5	6	8	9	1	7	4
9	8	1	4	5	7	6	2	3
4	7	3	9	1	2	5	8	6
5	9	2	8	3	6	4	1	7
8	1	6	7	4	5	9	3	2

8/5

9	1	8	6	3	4	2	7	5
6	3	4	5	7	2	1	9	8
5	2	7	1	9	8	6	3	4
2	6	9	3	8	5	7	4	1
7	5	1	2	4	9	8	6	3
8	4	3	7	1	6	5	2	9
3	9	5	8	6	7	4	1	2
4	8	6	9	2	1	3	5	7
1	7	2	4	5	3	9	8	6

8/6

7	9	2	8	1	3	6	5	4
3	1	6	4	5	7	8	2	9
5	4	8	6	2	9	7	1	3
8	7	1	5	9	4	2	3	6
4	5	9	3	6	2	1	8	7
6	2	3	1	7	8	4	9	5
1	8	5	9	4	6	3	7	2
9	6	7	2	3	1	5	4	8
2	3	4	7	8	5	9	6	1

8/7

4	6	3	1	2	8	9	5	7
9	8	5	7	3	6	1	2	4
7	1	2	9	5	4	3	6	8
1	2	7	5	8	9	4	3	6
5	4	8	3	6	1	2	7	9
3	9	6	2	4	7	5	8	1
8	5	4	6	9	2	7	1	3
2	7	9	8	1	3	6	4	5
6	3	1	4	7	5	8	9	2

8/8

6	5	9	3	2	1	4	7	8
2	1	8	7	4	9	5	3	6
3	4	7	6	5	8	2	9	1
5	7	2	8	6	3	9	1	4
4	3	1	2	9	5	6	8	7
9	8	6	1	7	4	3	5	2
7	9	3	4	1	2	8	6	5
1	2	5	9	8	6	7	4	3
8	6	4	5	3	7	1	2	9

89

1	9	4	7	8	2	5	3	6
5	6	7	9	4	3	8	1	2
8	2	3	1	5	6	7	4	9
6	8	2	5	1	7	4	9	3
7	4	1	3	9	8	6	2	5
3	5	9	6	2	4	1	7	8
9	3	5	4	6	1	2	8	7
2	1	6	8	7	9	3	5	4
4	7	8	2	3	5	9	6	1

90

2	1	5	9	7	6	4	8	3
4	8	9	3	1	5	7	2	6
3	7	6	2	4	8	9	5	1
8	2	7	5	6	3	1	4	9
5	3	4	7	9	1	8	6	2
9	6	1	4	8	2	5	3	7
6	9	2	8	5	7	3	1	4
7	5	3	1	2	4	6	9	8
1	4	8	6	3	9	2	7	5

91

9	7	8	4	2	3	1	5	6
5	6	1	8	7	9	4	3	2
2	3	4	5	6	1	7	8	9
4	5	7	3	1	6	2	9	8
3	1	9	2	8	7	5	6	4
6	8	2	9	5	4	3	1	7
1	2	6	7	9	5	8	4	3
8	4	5	6	3	2	9	7	1
7	9	3	1	4	8	6	2	5

92

3	2	6	4	7	5	1	9	8
9	4	8	1	3	6	2	7	5
1	5	7	9	8	2	4	3	6
2	7	3	5	9	8	6	1	4
4	8	5	3	6	1	9	2	7
6	1	9	7	2	4	8	5	3
7	6	2	8	1	3	5	4	9
5	3	1	6	4	9	7	8	2
8	9	4	2	5	7	3	6	1

93

9	5	8	1	7	3	2	6	4
2	3	7	4	6	9	8	1	5
4	6	1	2	8	5	3	9	7
1	4	6	9	2	7	5	8	3
7	8	5	3	1	6	9	4	2
3	2	9	5	4	8	6	7	1
8	1	3	7	9	2	4	5	6
5	9	4	6	3	1	7	2	8
6	7	2	8	5	4	1	3	9

94

5	6	2	4	1	9	8	3	7
9	1	7	5	3	8	4	6	2
8	3	4	6	7	2	9	1	5
2	8	3	7	5	1	6	9	4
4	7	5	8	9	6	3	2	1
6	9	1	2	4	3	7	5	8
7	5	9	3	2	4	1	8	6
3	4	6	1	8	5	2	7	9
1	2	8	9	6	7	5	4	3

95

8	3	1	9	6	7	5	4	2
7	9	4	1	5	2	3	8	6
6	5	2	3	4	8	9	1	7
9	2	6	8	3	5	4	7	1
4	1	3	7	9	6	2	5	8
5	8	7	4	2	1	6	3	9
1	4	9	6	7	3	8	2	5
3	7	5	2	8	9	1	6	4
2	6	8	5	1	4	7	9	3

96

7	4	2	3	6	9	5	8	1
9	5	8	4	1	7	6	2	3
3	6	1	5	2	8	7	4	9
2	7	6	1	9	5	8	3	4
1	8	4	6	3	2	9	5	7
5	9	3	7	8	4	1	6	2
4	3	7	9	5	6	2	1	8
8	1	5	2	7	3	4	9	6
6	2	9	8	4	1	3	7	5

97

3	9	6	2	4	8	1	5	7
4	7	2	9	1	5	6	3	8
8	1	5	7	6	3	4	2	9
7	4	1	5	8	2	3	9	6
6	2	3	1	7	9	5	8	4
5	8	9	4	3	6	7	1	2
2	3	7	8	5	4	9	6	1
9	6	4	3	2	1	8	7	5
1	5	8	6	9	7	2	4	3

98

3	5	9	2	1	8	4	6	7
4	8	7	9	5	6	1	3	2
1	2	6	7	4	3	9	8	5
7	4	8	1	3	2	5	9	6
2	9	1	6	8	5	3	7	4
5	6	3	4	7	9	8	2	1
9	1	2	3	6	4	7	5	8
8	3	4	5	2	7	6	1	9
6	7	5	8	9	1	2	4	3

99

6	8	2	5	3	9	7	4	1
1	9	7	6	8	4	5	2	3
4	5	3	1	7	2	8	9	6
2	6	8	4	5	7	3	1	9
5	4	1	9	6	3	2	8	7
3	7	9	8	2	1	6	5	4
7	3	4	2	1	5	9	6	8
9	2	6	7	4	8	1	3	5
8	1	5	3	9	6	4	7	2

100

9	4	6	2	5	3	7	8	1
7	3	8	4	6	1	9	5	2
2	1	5	9	7	8	6	4	3
5	6	7	1	4	2	3	9	8
3	2	9	7	8	5	4	1	6
4	8	1	3	9	6	5	2	7
1	9	2	5	3	7	8	6	4
6	7	4	8	2	9	1	3	5
8	5	3	6	1	4	2	7	9

101

4	5	1	8	3	6	9	2	7
8	9	7	2	4	1	3	6	5
3	6	2	5	7	9	8	4	1
5	8	9	6	1	3	4	7	2
1	2	4	9	5	7	6	8	3
6	7	3	4	8	2	1	5	9
2	1	8	3	6	5	7	9	4
9	3	6	7	2	4	5	1	8
7	4	5	1	9	8	2	3	6

102

2	5	4	8	7	9	1	3	6
8	7	1	3	6	4	2	9	5
9	3	6	5	1	2	8	4	7
3	6	7	2	4	5	9	1	8
1	9	2	7	8	3	6	5	4
4	8	5	6	9	1	3	7	2
6	2	9	1	5	7	4	8	3
5	4	3	9	2	8	7	6	1
7	1	8	4	3	6	5	2	9

103

5	8	3	9	1	2	4	6	7
2	9	7	5	4	6	8	1	3
6	4	1	8	3	7	9	2	5
1	3	5	2	7	8	6	9	4
4	6	9	3	5	1	2	7	8
8	7	2	4	6	9	5	3	1
3	2	6	7	8	5	1	4	9
9	5	4	1	2	3	7	8	6
7	1	8	6	9	4	3	5	2

104

3	9	6	5	1	7	4	2	8
1	7	4	2	8	6	5	9	3
2	8	5	4	9	3	1	7	6
4	5	9	8	3	1	2	6	7
8	3	7	6	2	5	9	4	1
6	2	1	7	4	9	3	8	5
9	1	2	3	6	8	7	5	4
5	6	3	9	7	4	8	1	2
7	4	8	1	5	2	6	3	9

105

7	9	5	4	2	3	8	1	6
2	8	4	1	9	6	3	7	5
6	1	3	8	5	7	9	2	4
9	7	6	3	1	5	4	8	2
5	3	8	2	7	4	1	6	9
1	4	2	6	8	9	5	3	7
8	6	7	5	4	1	2	9	3
3	5	1	9	6	2	7	4	8
4	2	9	7	3	8	6	5	1

106

4	3	9	2	8	5	6	1	7
7	8	2	3	6	1	4	5	9
5	1	6	4	7	9	2	3	8
6	9	7	1	3	2	8	4	5
3	5	1	8	4	7	9	6	2
8	2	4	5	9	6	1	7	3
1	6	5	9	2	3	7	8	4
2	7	8	6	5	4	3	9	1
9	4	3	7	1	8	5	2	6

107

7	8	1	5	9	6	2	4	3
3	6	2	7	8	4	9	5	1
4	5	9	1	2	3	7	6	8
5	2	6	8	7	9	1	3	4
8	1	4	3	5	2	6	7	9
9	3	7	6	4	1	8	2	5
1	7	3	9	6	5	4	8	2
2	9	8	4	3	7	5	1	6
6	4	5	2	1	8	3	9	7

108

8	9	2	7	6	4	1	5	3
3	6	5	1	2	9	4	8	7
1	7	4	8	3	5	6	9	2
9	4	3	2	1	6	8	7	5
7	5	6	4	9	8	3	2	1
2	1	8	3	5	7	9	4	6
5	8	1	6	4	2	7	3	9
6	2	7	9	8	3	5	1	4
4	3	9	5	7	1	2	6	8

109

3	9	1	6	7	8	2	5	4
4	2	7	3	1	5	6	8	9
6	5	8	9	2	4	1	7	3
5	8	6	2	4	3	7	9	1
7	1	9	5	8	6	3	4	2
2	4	3	7	9	1	5	6	8
1	6	4	8	3	7	9	2	5
9	3	5	4	6	2	8	1	7
8	7	2	1	5	9	4	3	6

110

3	7	1	8	9	6	4	2	5
2	4	5	1	3	7	8	9	6
6	9	8	2	4	5	7	1	3
5	2	6	7	1	8	3	4	9
7	8	9	4	5	3	1	6	2
4	1	3	9	6	2	5	7	8
8	6	4	3	7	9	2	5	1
9	3	7	5	2	1	6	8	4
1	5	2	6	8	4	9	3	7

111

2	7	5	6	4	9	3	1	8
9	4	3	1	8	2	6	7	5
1	6	8	3	7	5	9	4	2
3	9	7	4	2	6	5	8	1
6	8	4	5	9	1	7	2	3
5	2	1	8	3	7	4	6	9
4	1	2	7	5	3	8	9	6
8	5	9	2	6	4	1	3	7
7	3	6	9	1	8	2	5	4

112

1	5	6	4	8	7	2	3	9
9	7	4	2	5	3	1	6	8
8	2	3	9	1	6	7	5	4
7	9	1	6	3	4	5	8	2
4	3	5	8	2	1	9	7	6
6	8	2	5	7	9	3	4	1
5	1	9	3	6	8	4	2	7
3	4	8	7	9	2	6	1	5
2	6	7	1	4	5	8	9	3

113

4	8	5	9	3	7	6	2	1
2	6	9	1	8	4	3	5	7
3	1	7	6	2	5	9	8	4
1	9	3	2	7	8	4	6	5
5	7	8	3	4	6	1	9	2
6	2	4	5	9	1	7	3	8
7	5	1	8	6	3	2	4	9
9	4	6	7	5	2	8	1	3
8	3	2	4	1	9	5	7	6

114

9	2	4	7	8	6	5	1	3
5	3	6	9	1	2	7	4	8
8	1	7	5	3	4	6	2	9
2	9	3	4	6	5	1	8	7
1	4	5	8	9	7	3	6	2
7	6	8	3	2	1	9	5	4
6	7	9	1	4	8	2	3	5
3	8	1	2	5	9	4	7	6
4	5	2	6	7	3	8	9	1

115

7	4	6	8	9	5	3	2	1
2	8	3	1	6	4	7	9	5
1	9	5	3	7	2	4	8	6
8	7	9	4	3	1	5	6	2
4	3	2	6	5	8	9	1	7
5	6	1	9	2	7	8	3	4
6	2	8	5	4	3	1	7	9
3	5	7	2	1	9	6	4	8
9	1	4	7	8	6	2	5	3

116

7	9	2	8	4	1	5	3	6
5	8	6	2	7	3	1	4	9
4	1	3	5	6	9	7	2	8
8	4	5	6	3	7	9	1	2
1	3	7	9	2	8	4	6	5
2	6	9	4	1	5	8	7	3
9	7	1	3	8	2	6	5	4
3	5	4	1	9	6	2	8	7
6	2	8	7	5	4	3	9	1

117

6	3	2	5	8	4	1	7	9
8	4	1	9	7	2	3	6	5
9	5	7	1	3	6	2	8	4
7	1	4	3	2	8	5	9	6
5	9	6	7	4	1	8	2	3
2	8	3	6	5	9	7	4	1
1	6	5	8	9	7	4	3	2
3	2	8	4	6	5	9	1	7
4	7	9	2	1	3	6	5	8

118

2	8	1	9	4	6	3	5	7
7	3	6	8	5	1	4	9	2
4	5	9	2	3	7	1	8	6
9	7	2	1	6	4	5	3	8
8	1	5	3	2	9	7	6	4
6	4	3	5	7	8	9	2	1
3	9	4	6	1	2	8	7	5
5	2	7	4	8	3	6	1	9
1	6	8	7	9	5	2	4	3

119

9	2	6	3	7	1	4	5	8
5	8	4	2	6	9	1	3	7
1	7	3	8	4	5	2	9	6
4	9	8	6	1	3	7	2	5
2	3	7	4	5	8	6	1	9
6	5	1	7	9	2	8	4	3
8	1	9	5	2	6	3	7	4
3	4	5	1	8	7	9	6	2
7	6	2	9	3	4	5	8	1

120

1	9	5	8	7	6	4	2	3
4	7	3	2	5	9	8	6	1
6	2	8	1	4	3	9	5	7
8	1	9	7	3	2	6	4	5
5	4	2	6	1	8	3	7	9
7	3	6	5	9	4	2	1	8
3	5	4	9	2	7	1	8	6
2	6	1	3	8	5	7	9	4
9	8	7	4	6	1	5	3	2

121

3	7	6	2	5	4	8	9	1
2	9	5	1	8	6	7	4	3
8	1	4	7	3	9	6	5	2
7	8	9	6	2	3	5	1	4
4	5	3	8	7	1	9	2	6
6	2	1	9	4	5	3	8	7
9	6	2	5	1	7	4	3	8
1	4	7	3	9	8	2	6	5
5	3	8	4	6	2	1	7	9

122

3	7	9	8	5	2	6	1	4
4	5	2	6	9	1	7	8	3
1	8	6	4	7	3	5	2	9
6	4	3	5	8	7	2	9	1
2	9	7	1	6	4	3	5	8
8	1	5	3	2	9	4	7	6
7	6	4	2	1	8	9	3	5
9	3	8	7	4	5	1	6	2
5	2	1	9	3	6	8	4	7

123

4	1	9	7	2	3	6	8	5
8	5	2	9	6	1	7	3	4
3	7	6	8	5	4	9	1	2
5	9	8	6	1	7	2	4	3
2	6	4	5	3	9	8	7	1
7	3	1	2	4	8	5	9	6
9	4	5	1	8	6	3	2	7
1	2	7	3	9	5	4	6	8
6	8	3	4	7	2	1	5	9

124

3	8	5	6	4	2	9	1	7
7	4	9	1	3	5	6	2	8
2	1	6	8	9	7	4	5	3
6	3	1	7	5	9	2	8	4
9	2	4	3	8	1	5	7	6
5	7	8	4	2	6	1	3	9
4	5	7	2	6	8	3	9	1
8	6	2	9	1	3	7	4	5
1	9	3	5	7	4	8	6	2

125

8	6	3	2	9	1	7	5	4
9	2	4	3	5	7	6	1	8
5	7	1	4	6	8	3	2	9
3	8	2	7	4	9	1	6	5
1	4	9	6	2	5	8	3	7
7	5	6	1	8	3	4	9	2
4	1	7	9	3	2	5	8	6
6	9	8	5	1	4	2	7	3
2	3	5	8	7	6	9	4	1

126

3	8	4	6	7	5	2	9	1
6	9	5	2	1	3	4	8	7
1	7	2	8	4	9	6	5	3
4	5	6	3	9	8	7	1	2
9	3	1	7	2	4	8	6	5
8	2	7	5	6	1	9	3	4
7	1	3	9	8	2	5	4	6
5	6	9	4	3	7	1	2	8
2	4	8	1	5	6	3	7	9

127

4	9	2	1	3	7	8	6	5
6	5	8	2	4	9	3	1	7
7	3	1	5	8	6	4	2	9
3	2	9	8	6	5	7	4	1
5	4	6	7	1	3	2	9	8
8	1	7	9	2	4	5	3	6
9	6	3	4	7	8	1	5	2
1	8	4	6	5	2	9	7	3
2	7	5	3	9	1	6	8	4

128

4	8	6	7	5	2	9	1	3
2	3	7	1	8	9	5	4	6
9	5	1	3	4	6	7	8	2
3	9	5	6	1	4	2	7	8
6	7	2	8	9	3	1	5	4
8	1	4	5	2	7	3	6	9
7	6	9	4	3	1	8	2	5
1	2	8	9	6	5	4	3	7
5	4	3	2	7	8	6	9	1

129

1	7	6	4	2	5	9	3	8
4	8	3	6	1	9	5	7	2
9	5	2	3	7	8	4	6	1
6	9	8	1	5	7	3	2	4
7	4	1	2	3	6	8	9	5
2	3	5	9	8	4	7	1	6
3	6	4	5	9	1	2	8	7
5	2	7	8	6	3	1	4	9
8	1	9	7	4	2	6	5	3

130

6	4	5	8	3	9	7	1	2
2	7	8	4	1	6	3	5	9
3	1	9	2	5	7	8	4	6
8	5	2	1	4	3	9	6	7
9	6	4	5	7	8	2	3	1
7	3	1	9	6	2	4	8	5
5	9	3	7	8	1	6	2	4
4	2	6	3	9	5	1	7	8
1	8	7	6	2	4	5	9	3

131

3	9	2	1	4	6	7	5	8
7	5	8	9	3	2	1	4	6
1	6	4	5	7	8	3	2	9
2	4	7	8	9	3	6	1	5
9	1	6	2	5	4	8	7	3
8	3	5	6	1	7	2	9	4
4	8	9	3	2	1	5	6	7
5	2	3	7	6	9	4	8	1
6	7	1	4	8	5	9	3	2

132

4	7	3	2	5	6	8	9	1
8	1	9	4	7	3	5	6	2
2	6	5	8	1	9	7	3	4
3	9	7	6	4	5	1	2	8
5	4	1	3	8	2	6	7	9
6	2	8	1	9	7	4	5	3
1	5	6	9	2	8	3	4	7
7	8	2	5	3	4	9	1	6
9	3	4	7	6	1	2	8	5

133

1	4	6	3	9	2	7	5	8
2	7	9	8	5	1	3	4	6
8	3	5	4	6	7	2	9	1
4	9	2	5	8	3	6	1	7
7	1	8	9	2	6	5	3	4
6	5	3	1	7	4	9	8	2
3	6	4	2	1	9	8	7	5
5	2	1	7	3	8	4	6	9
9	8	7	6	4	5	1	2	3

134

1	4	2	9	8	6	7	3	5
8	3	5	4	7	1	9	6	2
9	7	6	5	3	2	1	8	4
7	9	1	2	6	8	4	5	3
5	2	3	1	4	9	6	7	8
4	6	8	7	5	3	2	9	1
3	1	9	8	2	7	5	4	6
2	8	4	6	9	5	3	1	7
6	5	7	3	1	4	8	2	9

135

2	5	3	7	9	1	8	4	6
7	4	8	2	5	6	3	1	9
9	1	6	8	3	4	5	7	2
4	6	7	5	8	2	1	9	3
1	9	2	6	4	3	7	5	8
3	8	5	9	1	7	2	6	4
5	3	1	4	2	9	6	8	7
6	2	9	1	7	8	4	3	5
8	7	4	3	6	5	9	2	1

136

3	4	5	6	1	9	7	2	8
7	8	6	2	4	3	5	9	1
2	1	9	7	8	5	6	4	3
8	6	7	3	5	4	9	1	2
5	9	1	8	2	7	3	6	4
4	2	3	9	6	1	8	5	7
9	5	2	4	7	8	1	3	6
1	7	4	5	3	6	2	8	9
6	3	8	1	9	2	4	7	5

137

8	2	6	9	1	5	7	3	4
7	5	1	4	3	6	2	8	9
3	9	4	2	8	7	6	5	1
4	3	2	1	5	8	9	6	7
1	7	8	6	9	4	3	2	5
9	6	5	7	2	3	1	4	8
6	8	7	3	4	1	5	9	2
5	1	9	8	6	2	4	7	3
2	4	3	5	7	9	8	1	6

138

4	8	9	7	6	2	1	3	5
2	5	1	8	4	3	9	7	6
3	7	6	5	9	1	2	8	4
8	1	2	4	5	6	7	9	3
5	9	3	1	7	8	6	4	2
7	6	4	3	2	9	5	1	8
1	2	5	9	3	4	8	6	7
9	3	7	6	8	5	4	2	1
6	4	8	2	1	7	3	5	9

139

3	9	4	2	7	8	1	6	5
5	1	2	6	9	4	7	8	3
7	8	6	5	3	1	2	4	9
1	3	5	8	4	2	9	7	6
6	2	9	3	5	7	8	1	4
4	7	8	1	6	9	5	3	2
2	5	7	4	8	6	3	9	1
9	4	1	7	2	3	6	5	8
8	6	3	9	1	5	4	2	7

140

5	3	2	7	9	6	1	4	8
7	1	9	4	8	2	5	3	6
6	4	8	5	1	3	9	2	7
3	5	6	8	4	9	7	1	2
4	8	7	1	2	5	6	9	3
2	9	1	3	6	7	8	5	4
9	2	5	6	3	8	4	7	1
8	7	4	2	5	1	3	6	9
1	6	3	9	7	4	2	8	5

141

9	6	8	1	4	2	5	3	7
1	2	7	5	3	8	6	9	4
4	5	3	7	9	6	1	8	2
3	7	6	8	1	9	4	2	5
2	4	5	3	6	7	9	1	8
8	1	9	4	2	5	3	7	6
5	3	4	2	8	1	7	6	9
6	8	1	9	7	4	2	5	3
7	9	2	6	5	3	8	4	1

142

7	1	6	8	5	4	3	9	2
2	4	3	1	7	9	6	8	5
9	8	5	2	3	6	1	4	7
1	6	7	9	8	2	5	3	4
4	3	2	7	6	5	9	1	8
8	5	9	3	4	1	7	2	6
6	9	1	5	2	8	4	7	3
5	7	8	4	1	3	2	6	9
3	2	4	6	9	7	8	5	1

143

1	7	6	5	4	8	2	9	3
5	2	3	1	9	6	4	7	8
8	4	9	7	3	2	5	6	1
7	1	2	9	6	4	3	8	5
6	3	5	8	7	1	9	4	2
4	9	8	3	2	5	6	1	7
3	6	1	4	5	7	8	2	9
9	8	4	2	1	3	7	5	6
2	5	7	6	8	9	1	3	4

144

3	5	9	1	8	2	4	7	6
7	2	6	4	9	5	1	8	3
8	4	1	6	3	7	9	2	5
1	9	3	7	5	4	8	6	2
2	7	8	9	6	3	5	4	1
4	6	5	2	1	8	7	3	9
5	8	4	3	2	9	6	1	7
6	3	7	5	4	1	2	9	8
9	1	2	8	7	6	3	5	4

145

5	3	6	8	9	7	2	1	4
4	7	9	5	2	1	3	8	6
2	1	8	3	6	4	5	7	9
9	2	4	7	3	6	1	5	8
1	5	7	4	8	2	9	6	3
8	6	3	9	1	5	4	2	7
7	9	2	1	4	8	6	3	5
6	4	5	2	7	3	8	9	1
3	8	1	6	5	9	7	4	2

146

8	1	9	4	2	5	3	7	6
2	3	6	8	7	1	5	4	9
5	4	7	3	6	9	2	1	8
1	2	5	9	8	7	6	3	4
4	7	3	2	5	6	9	8	1
6	9	8	1	3	4	7	5	2
7	8	4	6	9	3	1	2	5
3	6	1	5	4	2	8	9	7
9	5	2	7	1	8	4	6	3

147

6	7	5	9	1	4	3	8	2
1	9	3	7	2	8	4	6	5
8	2	4	6	5	3	7	1	9
5	8	2	3	6	9	1	4	7
9	3	7	4	8	1	2	5	6
4	1	6	2	7	5	8	9	3
7	4	8	5	9	2	6	3	1
2	5	1	8	3	6	9	7	4
3	6	9	1	4	7	5	2	8

148

8	4	5	7	9	2	6	1	3
6	9	7	3	1	4	2	8	5
1	2	3	8	6	5	7	4	9
4	7	1	9	2	8	5	3	6
2	3	6	4	5	1	8	9	7
9	5	8	6	7	3	1	2	4
5	8	4	1	3	6	9	7	2
3	6	9	2	8	7	4	5	1
7	1	2	5	4	9	3	6	8

149

3	9	5	7	4	2	8	1	6
6	4	7	9	8	1	2	5	3
1	8	2	6	5	3	7	4	9
4	3	6	2	9	8	5	7	1
5	7	8	4	1	6	3	9	2
9	2	1	5	3	7	4	6	8
2	1	9	8	7	4	6	3	5
7	6	3	1	2	5	9	8	4
8	5	4	3	6	9	1	2	7

150

1	5	9	3	4	2	6	7	8
6	2	7	5	9	8	3	4	1
8	4	3	7	6	1	9	2	5
5	6	2	9	1	3	4	8	7
7	9	8	4	5	6	2	1	3
4	3	1	2	8	7	5	9	6
9	8	5	1	3	4	7	6	2
2	1	4	6	7	5	8	3	9
3	7	6	8	2	9	1	5	4

151

7	8	9	5	1	3	4	2	6
5	4	1	6	2	7	3	8	9
3	2	6	9	8	4	7	5	1
9	5	4	2	3	6	8	1	7
2	7	3	8	5	1	6	9	4
6	1	8	7	4	9	5	3	2
8	6	7	3	9	2	1	4	5
4	3	2	1	7	5	9	6	8
1	9	5	4	6	8	2	7	3

152

6	4	8	3	2	7	9	5	1
9	1	7	8	6	5	2	3	4
5	3	2	9	1	4	7	6	8
2	6	4	1	7	9	3	8	5
8	9	5	2	4	3	1	7	6
3	7	1	6	5	8	4	2	9
4	5	6	7	9	2	8	1	3
7	8	9	5	3	1	6	4	2
1	2	3	4	8	6	5	9	7

153

1	9	4	6	2	8	7	5	3
3	2	5	1	7	9	4	8	6
8	6	7	3	4	5	2	9	1
2	8	1	5	6	3	9	7	4
9	4	6	7	8	1	5	3	2
5	7	3	2	9	4	6	1	8
6	5	8	4	1	7	3	2	9
7	1	2	9	3	6	8	4	5
4	3	9	8	5	2	1	6	7

154

3	6	7	1	8	4	9	2	5
9	5	4	6	7	2	1	3	8
8	2	1	9	5	3	6	4	7
5	7	6	2	9	8	4	1	3
2	3	8	5	4	1	7	9	6
1	4	9	7	3	6	5	8	2
6	9	3	4	2	7	8	5	1
7	8	5	3	1	9	2	6	4
4	1	2	8	6	5	3	7	9

155

9	5	7	2	3	1	4	6	8
6	4	3	7	8	5	9	1	2
8	2	1	9	4	6	3	7	5
4	7	9	1	6	8	2	5	3
5	3	2	4	7	9	1	8	6
1	8	6	3	5	2	7	9	4
3	6	4	5	9	7	8	2	1
7	1	5	8	2	3	6	4	9
2	9	8	6	1	4	5	3	7

156

5	6	8	9	2	3	7	4	1
2	9	7	1	5	4	6	8	3
1	4	3	7	6	8	2	9	5
3	8	1	6	7	2	9	5	4
6	7	9	5	4	1	8	3	2
4	5	2	3	8	9	1	7	6
8	2	5	4	9	6	3	1	7
9	3	4	2	1	7	5	6	8
7	1	6	8	3	5	4	2	9

157

7	5	4	3	8	6	9	2	1
1	3	6	5	2	9	4	7	8
9	8	2	1	4	7	5	3	6
8	9	1	6	7	4	2	5	3
5	2	3	9	1	8	7	6	4
6	4	7	2	3	5	1	8	9
4	7	5	8	6	1	3	9	2
2	1	8	7	9	3	6	4	5
3	6	9	4	5	2	8	1	7

158

8	3	4	2	6	1	5	9	7
7	1	6	5	3	9	8	4	2
5	9	2	7	8	4	1	3	6
9	5	7	3	1	2	4	6	8
1	6	3	8	4	5	2	7	9
2	4	8	6	9	7	3	5	1
6	2	9	1	5	3	7	8	4
4	7	5	9	2	8	6	1	3
3	8	1	4	7	6	9	2	5

159

8	6	5	4	2	9	3	7	1
1	7	9	6	8	3	2	5	4
3	2	4	5	1	7	6	9	8
6	5	2	8	3	4	7	1	9
7	1	8	2	9	6	5	4	3
4	9	3	7	5	1	8	6	2
5	4	1	3	6	8	9	2	7
2	3	7	9	4	5	1	8	6
9	8	6	1	7	2	4	3	5

160

9	3	2	8	4	6	7	5	1
1	5	7	9	3	2	8	4	6
8	4	6	7	1	5	9	3	2
6	1	4	5	2	7	3	8	9
2	7	3	1	9	8	4	6	5
5	8	9	4	6	3	1	2	7
7	9	8	2	5	4	6	1	3
4	6	5	3	7	1	2	9	8
3	2	1	6	8	9	5	7	4

161

8	3	1	6	7	4	9	5	2
2	5	4	3	9	1	8	7	6
9	6	7	5	2	8	4	1	3
5	2	8	9	3	7	6	4	1
4	7	9	1	6	2	3	8	5
3	1	6	4	8	5	2	9	7
7	8	5	2	4	3	1	6	9
1	9	3	8	5	6	7	2	4
6	4	2	7	1	9	5	3	8

162

7	5	6	3	1	2	8	9	4
1	2	3	9	4	8	7	6	5
8	9	4	5	7	6	1	2	3
2	4	7	6	5	9	3	1	8
6	8	9	4	3	1	2	5	7
5	3	1	8	2	7	9	4	6
3	6	2	7	9	5	4	8	1
4	1	8	2	6	3	5	7	9
9	7	5	1	8	4	6	3	2

163

9	1	2	7	4	6	3	5	8
4	7	6	5	3	8	2	1	9
5	3	8	9	2	1	4	6	7
2	8	4	1	7	5	9	3	6
6	9	7	2	8	3	1	4	5
3	5	1	4	6	9	8	7	2
1	6	3	8	5	2	7	9	4
8	4	9	6	1	7	5	2	3
7	2	5	3	9	4	6	8	1

164

5	4	6	8	2	1	9	7	3
2	3	1	9	5	7	8	4	6
9	7	8	4	3	6	5	1	2
4	6	5	1	8	2	7	3	9
3	8	9	7	6	5	4	2	1
1	2	7	3	9	4	6	8	5
7	5	3	2	4	9	1	6	8
6	1	2	5	7	8	3	9	4
8	9	4	6	1	3	2	5	7

165

9	5	4	1	2	3	8	6	7
7	8	3	4	6	5	9	1	2
2	6	1	7	8	9	3	4	5
6	7	8	3	5	4	1	2	9
3	2	9	8	1	6	7	5	4
4	1	5	9	7	2	6	8	3
5	3	2	6	9	1	4	7	8
8	4	6	5	3	7	2	9	1
1	9	7	2	4	8	5	3	6

166

5	9	3	8	4	6	7	2	1
2	7	1	5	9	3	6	8	4
4	6	8	2	7	1	3	5	9
6	8	4	3	2	9	5	1	7
1	2	9	7	5	4	8	6	3
7	3	5	6	1	8	9	4	2
3	5	7	1	8	2	4	9	6
9	1	6	4	3	5	2	7	8
8	4	2	9	6	7	1	3	5

167

2	6	7	1	4	3	9	5	8
8	9	5	7	6	2	4	3	1
3	1	4	9	5	8	2	7	6
7	5	6	8	3	4	1	9	2
4	3	9	2	7	1	6	8	5
1	8	2	5	9	6	7	4	3
6	7	3	4	2	5	8	1	9
9	2	1	3	8	7	5	6	4
5	4	8	6	1	9	3	2	7

168

7	4	9	1	6	3	2	8	5
6	1	2	4	8	5	7	3	9
3	8	5	9	7	2	4	6	1
8	7	6	5	3	4	9	1	2
2	9	3	7	1	6	5	4	8
4	5	1	2	9	8	6	7	3
5	2	7	8	4	1	3	9	6
1	3	4	6	2	9	8	5	7
9	6	8	3	5	7	1	2	4

169

5	9	8	7	1	6	2	3	4
7	4	1	9	2	3	8	5	6
2	6	3	5	8	4	7	9	1
9	8	5	1	4	2	6	7	3
1	3	2	8	6	7	5	4	9
6	7	4	3	5	9	1	2	8
3	5	9	6	7	8	4	1	2
4	1	6	2	9	5	3	8	7
8	2	7	4	3	1	9	6	5

170

9	4	2	7	3	6	5	8	1
3	7	6	1	8	5	4	9	2
8	5	1	4	9	2	7	6	3
5	1	8	9	6	7	3	2	4
4	3	9	2	5	8	1	7	6
2	6	7	3	4	1	9	5	8
7	8	3	6	1	9	2	4	5
6	2	4	5	7	3	8	1	9
1	9	5	8	2	4	6	3	7

171

2	7	6	1	4	3	5	8	9
8	4	9	2	5	7	3	1	6
5	1	3	9	6	8	2	4	7
4	8	2	5	1	9	7	6	3
7	3	1	6	8	2	9	5	4
9	6	5	3	7	4	1	2	8
3	5	4	8	9	1	6	7	2
6	2	7	4	3	5	8	9	1
1	9	8	7	2	6	4	3	5

172

3	5	4	1	6	2	8	7	9
6	9	7	3	4	8	5	2	1
1	8	2	7	5	9	3	6	4
4	2	3	5	7	6	1	9	8
5	7	8	9	1	3	2	4	6
9	6	1	8	2	4	7	3	5
7	1	6	2	9	5	4	8	3
8	4	5	6	3	7	9	1	2
2	3	9	4	8	1	6	5	7

173

9	7	8	2	6	3	5	4	1
3	2	6	5	4	1	8	9	7
5	4	1	8	7	9	2	3	6
2	3	5	4	1	8	6	7	9
8	6	7	3	9	2	1	5	4
4	1	9	6	5	7	3	2	8
1	5	3	7	8	4	9	6	2
7	8	2	9	3	6	4	1	5
6	9	4	1	2	5	7	8	3

174

9	2	3	4	5	1	8	7	6
8	7	4	6	3	2	5	1	9
6	1	5	9	8	7	2	4	3
7	4	2	1	9	5	3	6	8
3	5	6	2	4	8	1	9	7
1	9	8	7	6	3	4	2	5
2	3	7	8	1	9	6	5	4
5	6	9	3	2	4	7	8	1
4	8	1	5	7	6	9	3	2

175

5	9	6	2	4	8	1	7	3
7	3	1	6	9	5	8	4	2
2	8	4	7	1	3	6	9	5
4	6	7	3	8	1	5	2	9
9	5	2	4	6	7	3	8	1
3	1	8	9	5	2	7	6	4
6	2	5	1	7	4	9	3	8
1	7	3	8	2	9	4	5	6
8	4	9	5	3	6	2	1	7

176

7	1	4	3	8	5	6	2	9
2	3	6	7	1	9	5	4	8
8	9	5	4	2	6	3	1	7
1	8	9	2	6	3	4	7	5
4	7	3	1	5	8	2	9	6
5	6	2	9	7	4	8	3	1
9	5	7	8	4	2	1	6	3
6	4	1	5	3	7	9	8	2
3	2	8	6	9	1	7	5	4

177

4	9	3	8	6	1	7	2	5
2	7	5	9	4	3	8	1	6
6	8	1	7	2	5	9	3	4
8	5	9	2	7	4	1	6	3
7	3	2	1	9	6	5	4	8
1	4	6	5	3	8	2	9	7
3	1	7	6	5	2	4	8	9
5	6	8	4	1	9	3	7	2
9	2	4	3	8	7	6	5	1

178

2	5	3	7	4	6	9	1	8
8	9	1	5	3	2	6	4	7
6	4	7	9	8	1	3	5	2
5	6	2	8	1	9	7	3	4
4	3	9	2	5	7	8	6	1
1	7	8	3	6	4	5	2	9
3	2	4	6	7	8	1	9	5
9	8	6	1	2	5	4	7	3
7	1	5	4	9	3	2	8	6

179

2	3	7	1	6	9	8	5	4
6	5	1	4	3	8	7	9	2
4	9	8	5	7	2	3	1	6
7	1	3	8	4	6	9	2	5
8	4	9	2	5	3	6	7	1
5	2	6	7	9	1	4	8	3
3	8	2	6	1	7	5	4	9
9	7	5	3	2	4	1	6	8
1	6	4	9	8	5	2	3	7

180

8	9	1	5	2	3	6	7	4
3	6	4	1	9	7	5	2	8
7	2	5	4	8	6	3	9	1
2	5	6	8	1	9	7	4	3
1	8	7	3	6	4	9	5	2
9	4	3	2	7	5	1	8	6
4	7	2	6	5	1	8	3	9
6	3	9	7	4	8	2	1	5
5	1	8	9	3	2	4	6	7

181

9	2	5	4	8	6	7	3	1
4	8	7	2	3	1	9	5	6
3	1	6	9	7	5	8	4	2
7	3	4	1	2	9	6	8	5
8	6	2	7	5	4	3	1	9
5	9	1	8	6	3	4	2	7
1	5	8	3	9	7	2	6	4
2	4	9	6	1	8	5	7	3
6	7	3	5	4	2	1	9	8

182

8	1	2	6	3	7	9	5	4
3	5	6	4	1	9	7	8	2
9	4	7	2	8	5	6	3	1
5	8	4	7	6	3	1	2	9
6	9	3	1	5	2	8	4	7
7	2	1	9	4	8	3	6	5
4	6	9	8	2	1	5	7	3
2	7	5	3	9	6	4	1	8
1	3	8	5	7	4	2	9	6

183

9	8	6	7	2	5	4	1	3
5	3	1	4	8	9	6	2	7
2	7	4	3	1	6	9	5	8
1	5	7	9	6	3	8	4	2
8	9	3	2	4	1	7	6	5
6	4	2	8	5	7	3	9	1
3	2	5	6	7	4	1	8	9
4	1	9	5	3	8	2	7	6
7	6	8	1	9	2	5	3	4

184

3	6	4	5	9	1	7	8	2
2	1	8	3	4	7	6	9	5
5	7	9	6	2	8	3	4	1
4	8	2	9	1	3	5	6	7
7	5	1	8	6	4	9	2	3
9	3	6	2	7	5	4	1	8
8	9	5	1	3	6	2	7	4
1	2	7	4	5	9	8	3	6
6	4	3	7	8	2	1	5	9

185

7	1	4	6	3	8	9	5	2
8	5	9	2	7	4	3	1	6
3	6	2	5	9	1	8	7	4
6	9	5	4	8	7	2	3	1
4	2	8	3	1	6	7	9	5
1	7	3	9	2	5	6	4	8
9	4	7	1	6	2	5	8	3
2	8	1	7	5	3	4	6	9
5	3	6	8	4	9	1	2	7

186

8	9	6	7	3	1	2	5	4
5	2	4	9	8	6	3	1	7
7	3	1	4	2	5	9	6	8
4	7	2	1	9	8	6	3	5
3	1	9	5	6	7	8	4	2
6	8	5	3	4	2	1	7	9
2	6	3	8	7	4	5	9	1
1	4	8	6	5	9	7	2	3
9	5	7	2	1	3	4	8	6

187

6	4	9	3	5	7	8	2	1
5	7	8	1	6	2	3	4	9
1	2	3	8	4	9	6	7	5
2	8	1	4	9	3	5	6	7
4	3	7	6	1	5	2	9	8
9	5	6	2	7	8	4	1	3
8	6	4	7	3	1	9	5	2
3	1	5	9	2	6	7	8	4
7	9	2	5	8	4	1	3	6

188

5	3	1	4	2	7	8	6	9
8	2	4	9	6	5	7	1	3
9	6	7	3	1	8	4	2	5
7	9	3	1	5	6	2	8	4
4	5	6	8	9	2	3	7	1
1	8	2	7	3	4	9	5	6
6	1	8	2	4	3	5	9	7
3	7	9	5	8	1	6	4	2
2	4	5	6	7	9	1	3	8

189

6	7	9	8	2	4	5	1	3
3	5	8	1	6	7	4	9	2
2	4	1	5	9	3	6	8	7
5	3	4	2	1	6	8	7	9
1	8	6	3	7	9	2	4	5
7	9	2	4	8	5	1	3	6
9	2	3	6	4	8	7	5	1
8	1	5	7	3	2	9	6	4
4	6	7	9	5	1	3	2	8

190

9	2	5	1	6	3	8	7	4
8	3	7	4	5	2	6	1	9
6	1	4	9	7	8	5	2	3
2	5	8	3	4	9	7	6	1
4	7	9	5	1	6	2	3	8
3	6	1	8	2	7	9	4	5
1	4	6	2	9	5	3	8	7
7	9	3	6	8	4	1	5	2
5	8	2	7	3	1	4	9	6

191

3	7	6	2	9	4	5	8	1
9	5	4	1	6	8	7	2	3
1	8	2	5	3	7	6	4	9
6	9	7	3	4	1	2	5	8
2	4	8	6	5	9	1	3	7
5	3	1	8	7	2	9	6	4
7	1	5	4	8	6	3	9	2
8	2	3	9	1	5	4	7	6
4	6	9	7	2	3	8	1	5

192

3	8	5	6	7	9	4	1	2
9	6	4	1	2	3	8	7	5
7	1	2	8	5	4	3	6	9
1	7	3	2	6	5	9	8	4
6	2	8	9	4	1	7	5	3
5	4	9	3	8	7	6	2	1
2	9	1	7	3	6	5	4	8
4	3	7	5	1	8	2	9	6
8	5	6	4	9	2	1	3	7

193

2	8	4	5	9	1	6	3	7
1	7	5	2	3	6	9	8	4
6	9	3	4	7	8	5	1	2
9	3	1	8	2	4	7	6	5
5	4	7	1	6	9	3	2	8
8	2	6	3	5	7	1	4	9
3	5	9	6	4	2	8	7	1
7	1	2	9	8	3	4	5	6
4	6	8	7	1	5	2	9	3

194

3	9	7	4	5	2	1	8	6
4	8	1	7	9	6	5	3	2
5	2	6	8	3	1	4	7	9
1	6	3	2	8	9	7	4	5
7	4	2	1	6	5	8	9	3
8	5	9	3	4	7	2	6	1
9	3	8	5	2	4	6	1	7
6	7	5	9	1	8	3	2	4
2	1	4	6	7	3	9	5	8

195

3	1	7	5	4	9	8	6	2
8	9	2	6	1	7	4	5	3
4	5	6	3	8	2	9	7	1
6	4	5	1	2	3	7	9	8
2	3	8	7	9	4	5	1	6
1	7	9	8	6	5	2	3	4
9	8	3	2	5	1	6	4	7
5	6	1	4	7	8	3	2	9
7	2	4	9	3	6	1	8	5

196

3	7	4	6	8	5	9	1	2
5	6	1	2	3	9	4	8	7
9	8	2	4	1	7	3	6	5
2	5	7	8	4	6	1	3	9
4	1	9	7	2	3	8	5	6
8	3	6	5	9	1	7	2	4
7	9	8	1	6	2	5	4	3
1	2	5	3	7	4	6	9	8
6	4	3	9	5	8	2	7	1

197

3	7	6	5	1	9	2	8	4
9	5	8	4	2	7	6	1	3
2	1	4	3	8	6	7	9	5
4	9	7	8	6	2	3	5	1
1	6	2	9	3	5	4	7	8
5	8	3	1	7	4	9	2	6
8	2	9	6	4	1	5	3	7
7	4	1	2	5	3	8	6	9
6	3	5	7	9	8	1	4	2

198

4	6	9	7	1	3	8	5	2
1	5	8	2	4	6	3	9	7
2	3	7	9	8	5	6	4	1
3	1	5	6	9	4	7	2	8
8	2	6	1	5	7	4	3	9
9	7	4	8	3	2	5	1	6
5	8	2	4	7	1	9	6	3
6	9	3	5	2	8	1	7	4
7	4	1	3	6	9	2	8	5

199

1	3	4	6	5	9	8	2	7
9	8	6	4	7	2	3	5	1
7	2	5	8	3	1	9	6	4
6	4	2	5	9	3	7	1	8
8	1	7	2	6	4	5	3	9
5	9	3	1	8	7	2	4	6
3	5	9	7	1	6	4	8	2
2	7	1	3	4	8	6	9	5
4	6	8	9	2	5	1	7	3

200

6	8	2	1	5	4	9	3	7
7	3	5	8	2	9	4	6	1
9	1	4	7	6	3	5	8	2
2	6	9	5	3	7	1	4	8
8	7	1	4	9	6	2	5	3
5	4	3	2	1	8	6	7	9
3	2	6	9	7	5	8	1	4
1	5	8	3	4	2	7	9	6
4	9	7	6	8	1	3	2	5

201

9	7	2	4	3	6	8	5	1
6	3	5	2	8	1	7	9	4
8	4	1	9	5	7	3	6	2
2	5	7	6	4	9	1	3	8
1	6	8	5	2	3	9	4	7
4	9	3	1	7	8	5	2	6
3	2	9	8	1	4	6	7	5
5	1	6	7	9	2	4	8	3
7	8	4	3	6	5	2	1	9

202

9	7	6	3	5	4	8	1	2
4	8	5	1	2	6	9	3	7
3	1	2	9	8	7	5	4	6
5	6	7	8	1	2	3	9	4
2	9	8	6	4	3	7	5	1
1	3	4	5	7	9	6	2	8
6	2	3	7	9	1	4	8	5
8	4	9	2	6	5	1	7	3
7	5	1	4	3	8	2	6	9

203

3	2	6	8	4	9	5	7	1
1	9	7	5	3	2	4	8	6
8	4	5	6	1	7	9	2	3
9	3	2	7	8	1	6	5	4
5	6	4	2	9	3	7	1	8
7	8	1	4	5	6	2	3	9
4	1	9	3	2	5	8	6	7
6	5	8	1	7	4	3	9	2
2	7	3	9	6	8	1	4	5

204

2	4	6	9	5	8	1	3	7
7	9	8	3	1	6	4	2	5
3	1	5	2	4	7	9	6	8
9	5	3	6	7	4	2	8	1
1	7	4	8	3	2	6	5	9
6	8	2	5	9	1	7	4	3
5	6	9	7	2	3	8	1	4
4	2	7	1	8	5	3	9	6
8	3	1	4	6	9	5	7	2

205

9	7	6	3	5	4	1	2	8
4	5	2	7	8	1	9	3	6
8	3	1	6	2	9	5	7	4
3	8	5	9	1	7	4	6	2
1	2	9	8	4	6	7	5	3
6	4	7	2	3	5	8	9	1
7	9	8	1	6	2	3	4	5
2	1	4	5	9	3	6	8	7
5	6	3	4	7	8	2	1	9

206

7	1	8	4	9	3	6	2	5
3	5	9	2	6	8	7	1	4
2	4	6	1	7	5	8	9	3
8	3	2	6	4	1	9	5	7
6	7	1	5	8	9	4	3	2
5	9	4	7	3	2	1	6	8
1	8	3	9	5	4	2	7	6
4	2	7	3	1	6	5	8	9
9	6	5	8	2	7	3	4	1

207

7	1	2	5	4	8	9	3	6
6	3	8	1	2	9	7	4	5
9	5	4	6	7	3	1	2	8
1	4	5	8	9	6	3	7	2
8	2	6	7	3	4	5	1	9
3	7	9	2	1	5	6	8	4
5	8	1	4	6	7	2	9	3
4	9	7	3	5	2	8	6	1
2	6	3	9	8	1	4	5	7

208

6	1	3	8	4	9	7	2	5
2	8	7	6	3	5	4	9	1
4	5	9	1	2	7	8	6	3
8	3	2	5	9	4	6	1	7
5	9	1	2	7	6	3	8	4
7	4	6	3	8	1	2	5	9
9	6	4	7	5	8	1	3	2
1	2	5	4	6	3	9	7	8
3	7	8	9	1	2	5	4	6

209

1	2	3	4	5	8	7	9	6
8	4	5	6	7	9	3	2	1
9	6	7	3	1	2	4	5	8
6	1	2	7	3	5	9	8	4
4	5	8	9	2	6	1	3	7
3	7	9	8	4	1	5	6	2
5	8	4	1	6	3	2	7	9
2	9	1	5	8	7	6	4	3
7	3	6	2	9	4	8	1	5

210

4	5	1	7	3	8	9	6	2
3	6	8	1	9	2	4	7	5
9	7	2	4	6	5	8	1	3
1	4	9	2	7	6	3	5	8
6	2	5	3	8	4	7	9	1
7	8	3	9	5	1	2	4	6
8	1	4	6	2	9	5	3	7
5	9	7	8	1	3	6	2	4
2	3	6	5	4	7	1	8	9

211

3	4	9	6	8	5	2	7	1
6	2	7	1	9	4	3	8	5
5	1	8	2	7	3	6	9	4
7	8	5	3	4	9	1	6	2
1	3	4	7	6	2	8	5	9
2	9	6	8	5	1	7	4	3
8	5	2	4	1	7	9	3	6
9	7	3	5	2	6	4	1	8
4	6	1	9	3	8	5	2	7

212

6	4	9	7	2	1	5	8	3
8	1	3	9	5	4	7	6	2
5	7	2	3	8	6	1	9	4
4	6	8	2	3	7	9	1	5
1	9	7	8	4	5	2	3	6
2	3	5	6	1	9	4	7	8
3	5	1	4	9	8	6	2	7
7	2	4	1	6	3	8	5	9
9	8	6	5	7	2	3	4	1

213

2	5	9	3	4	7	1	8	6
3	8	1	9	5	6	4	7	2
4	7	6	2	1	8	9	5	3
5	3	7	8	2	1	6	4	9
9	6	8	5	3	4	7	2	1
1	2	4	7	6	9	5	3	8
6	4	2	1	7	3	8	9	5
7	9	3	6	8	5	2	1	4
8	1	5	4	9	2	3	6	7

214

8	9	5	4	6	2	1	7	3
1	3	7	8	5	9	4	6	2
6	2	4	1	7	3	5	9	8
7	8	9	3	1	6	2	4	5
5	4	3	2	8	7	6	1	9
2	1	6	9	4	5	3	8	7
3	5	8	6	9	1	7	2	4
4	7	1	5	2	8	9	3	6
9	6	2	7	3	4	8	5	1

215

6	9	3	2	5	8	7	4	1
2	7	4	9	3	1	5	8	6
5	8	1	6	4	7	3	9	2
4	5	9	7	1	3	2	6	8
1	6	7	8	2	4	9	3	5
8	3	2	5	9	6	4	1	7
7	4	5	1	8	9	6	2	3
9	1	6	3	7	2	8	5	4
3	2	8	4	6	5	1	7	9

216

7	2	5	3	4	6	1	9	8
4	3	9	1	8	5	7	2	6
1	8	6	9	7	2	5	3	4
6	1	2	5	9	3	4	8	7
5	7	4	6	2	8	3	1	9
3	9	8	7	1	4	6	5	2
9	6	3	8	5	7	2	4	1
8	4	7	2	3	1	9	6	5
2	5	1	4	6	9	8	7	3

217

4	6	1	7	5	8	3	2	9
7	5	3	9	4	2	1	8	6
2	9	8	6	1	3	4	7	5
5	3	2	8	6	9	7	4	1
1	8	6	3	7	4	5	9	2
9	4	7	5	2	1	6	3	8
3	2	4	1	9	5	8	6	7
8	7	5	2	3	6	9	1	4
6	1	9	4	8	7	2	5	3

218

3	8	7	2	4	1	5	9	6
1	2	9	6	8	5	3	7	4
5	6	4	7	9	3	2	1	8
4	7	5	9	1	8	6	3	2
9	3	2	5	6	7	4	8	1
8	1	6	3	2	4	7	5	9
2	5	1	4	3	9	8	6	7
6	9	3	8	7	2	1	4	5
7	4	8	1	5	6	9	2	3

219

9	4	3	8	2	7	5	6	1
6	1	8	5	4	9	7	3	2
7	2	5	6	1	3	9	8	4
5	3	2	1	6	8	4	7	9
4	8	6	7	9	5	1	2	3
1	7	9	2	3	4	6	5	8
8	6	1	4	5	2	3	9	7
2	9	4	3	7	6	8	1	5
3	5	7	9	8	1	2	4	6

220

5	6	2	1	8	7	4	3	9
8	7	1	4	9	3	5	6	2
3	9	4	6	5	2	7	8	1
4	3	8	7	6	9	1	2	5
1	5	7	3	2	8	6	9	4
6	2	9	5	4	1	3	7	8
9	1	6	2	3	4	8	5	7
2	4	3	8	7	5	9	1	6
7	8	5	9	1	6	2	4	3

221

8	9	5	4	2	3	7	1	6
3	6	7	9	8	1	5	2	4
4	1	2	6	5	7	9	8	3
7	8	3	1	6	9	4	5	2
2	4	6	8	7	5	1	3	9
1	5	9	2	3	4	8	6	7
5	2	4	3	9	8	6	7	1
9	3	8	7	1	6	2	4	5
6	7	1	5	4	2	3	9	8

222

3	8	7	9	5	6	4	1	2
2	9	5	1	3	4	7	6	8
1	4	6	8	2	7	3	9	5
7	5	9	6	8	1	2	3	4
4	1	3	2	9	5	8	7	6
8	6	2	4	7	3	1	5	9
9	3	1	5	4	2	6	8	7
5	7	4	3	6	8	9	2	1
6	2	8	7	1	9	5	4	3

223

5	6	2	9	4	7	1	3	8
7	1	3	2	6	8	4	5	9
8	9	4	5	3	1	6	7	2
6	3	7	8	5	9	2	4	1
1	2	9	6	7	4	3	8	5
4	5	8	3	1	2	7	9	6
2	4	5	7	8	6	9	1	3
9	8	1	4	2	3	5	6	7
3	7	6	1	9	5	8	2	4

224

2	9	7	6	3	8	1	5	4
4	5	8	9	1	2	3	7	6
6	3	1	5	7	4	8	2	9
8	6	5	1	4	7	9	3	2
7	2	9	8	5	3	4	6	1
1	4	3	2	9	6	5	8	7
3	1	6	7	8	9	2	4	5
9	8	2	4	6	5	7	1	3
5	7	4	3	2	1	6	9	8

25

8	5	4	2	3	1	9	7	6
6	9	2	8	5	7	3	4	1
1	3	7	4	9	6	5	8	2
3	7	5	9	1	4	6	2	8
4	1	6	5	2	8	7	3	9
9	2	8	6	7	3	4	1	5
5	6	3	1	4	2	8	9	7
2	4	9	7	8	5	1	6	3
7	8	1	3	6	9	2	5	4

26

3	1	5	2	6	7	8	4	9
7	4	6	1	9	8	3	2	5
8	9	2	5	4	3	6	1	7
2	7	9	6	3	1	4	5	8
6	8	1	4	5	2	7	9	3
5	3	4	8	7	9	2	6	1
4	2	3	9	8	5	1	7	6
9	6	8	7	1	4	5	3	2
1	5	7	3	2	6	9	8	4

27

6	9	8	1	7	2	4	3	5
3	5	4	8	9	6	7	2	1
2	1	7	5	3	4	8	6	9
8	6	9	3	2	5	1	4	7
1	7	5	4	6	8	2	9	3
4	3	2	9	1	7	6	5	8
5	2	3	6	8	1	9	7	4
7	4	1	2	5	9	3	8	6
9	8	6	7	4	3	5	1	2

28

1	9	3	6	4	2	5	7	8
5	8	7	1	9	3	4	6	2
6	4	2	7	5	8	1	3	9
3	6	9	4	8	7	2	1	5
4	5	8	2	1	6	7	9	3
2	7	1	9	3	5	6	8	4
9	3	6	5	2	1	8	4	7
7	2	4	8	6	9	3	5	1
8	1	5	3	7	4	9	2	6

29

4	7	1	3	6	2	9	8	5
3	6	9	8	5	7	4	1	2
2	5	8	4	1	9	7	3	6
7	4	6	1	3	8	5	2	9
5	8	2	7	9	6	1	4	3
1	9	3	5	2	4	8	6	7
8	3	7	2	4	5	6	9	1
6	1	5	9	8	3	2	7	4
9	2	4	6	7	1	3	5	8

30

7	6	2	4	3	9	8	1	5
1	9	4	5	6	8	3	7	2
3	5	8	2	1	7	4	6	9
6	3	7	8	2	4	9	5	1
9	4	5	3	7	1	6	2	8
8	2	1	6	9	5	7	4	3
4	8	6	9	5	2	1	3	7
5	7	9	1	4	3	2	8	6
2	1	3	7	8	6	5	9	4

31

9	7	2	1	8	6	3	5	4
4	6	8	2	3	5	7	9	1
1	3	5	4	9	7	8	6	2
2	9	6	5	7	1	4	8	3
7	1	3	9	4	8	5	2	6
8	5	4	3	6	2	9	1	7
6	2	7	8	5	3	1	4	9
3	8	9	6	1	4	2	7	5
5	4	1	7	2	9	6	3	8

32

3	9	5	6	7	8	1	2	4
2	6	8	1	4	5	9	3	7
4	7	1	9	2	3	8	5	6
6	3	9	2	1	4	7	8	5
8	5	4	3	6	7	2	1	9
7	1	2	8	5	9	4	6	3
1	2	3	7	9	6	5	4	8
9	4	6	5	8	1	3	7	2
5	8	7	4	3	2	6	9	1

233

4	1	7	3	5	8	9	6	2
9	6	2	1	4	7	5	3	8
8	5	3	9	6	2	1	7	4
1	7	4	5	8	3	6	2	9
3	2	6	4	9	1	7	8	5
5	8	9	2	7	6	3	4	1
2	9	1	7	3	4	8	5	6
6	3	5	8	2	9	4	1	7
7	4	8	6	1	5	2	9	3

234

9	4	7	1	5	6	3	2	8
3	8	5	4	2	7	6	9	1
6	1	2	9	8	3	7	5	4
4	6	9	8	7	5	2	1	3
1	2	8	3	4	9	5	6	7
7	5	3	2	6	1	8	4	9
2	9	6	7	3	4	1	8	5
8	3	4	5	1	2	9	7	6
5	7	1	6	9	8	4	3	2

235

8	5	2	1	6	4	9	3	7
6	1	4	3	9	7	8	5	2
7	3	9	5	8	2	1	4	6
1	7	3	2	4	9	5	6	8
2	9	8	6	5	3	4	7	1
4	6	5	8	7	1	3	2	9
9	2	1	4	3	6	7	8	5
5	4	6	7	1	8	2	9	3
3	8	7	9	2	5	6	1	4

236

4	1	2	8	6	3	5	9	7
8	3	9	5	7	4	2	1	6
5	6	7	1	9	2	4	8	3
1	9	4	6	5	7	8	3	2
6	2	8	4	3	1	7	5	9
3	7	5	9	2	8	1	6	4
7	8	6	3	4	5	9	2	1
9	4	1	2	8	6	3	7	5
2	5	3	7	1	9	6	4	8

237

2	1	9	8	5	6	7	4	3
3	5	7	1	9	4	2	6	8
8	6	4	7	3	2	1	9	5
6	7	1	2	4	5	8	3	9
9	8	2	6	1	3	5	7	4
4	3	5	9	8	7	6	2	1
5	2	8	4	6	9	3	1	7
7	4	3	5	2	1	9	8	6
1	9	6	3	7	8	4	5	2

238

4	2	5	1	9	3	7	8	6
9	8	7	2	4	6	1	5	3
6	3	1	7	5	8	9	4	2
2	9	4	3	6	7	8	1	5
8	5	6	9	1	4	2	3	7
7	1	3	5	8	2	6	9	4
3	7	9	4	2	1	5	6	8
5	4	8	6	7	9	3	2	1
1	6	2	8	3	5	4	7	9

239

7	1	2	8	3	4	6	9	5
5	4	9	6	1	7	3	2	8
8	6	3	2	5	9	1	7	4
1	2	5	4	6	3	7	8	9
4	9	6	7	8	2	5	1	3
3	8	7	5	9	1	4	6	2
6	5	4	1	2	8	9	3	7
2	3	1	9	7	5	8	4	6
9	7	8	3	4	6	2	5	1

240

9	7	4	5	3	8	6	2	1
3	8	6	1	9	2	4	5	7
2	5	1	7	6	4	3	9	8
7	3	9	4	2	5	1	8	6
1	4	8	9	7	6	5	3	2
5	6	2	3	8	1	7	4	9
8	1	5	2	4	7	9	6	3
6	9	7	8	5	3	2	1	4
4	2	3	6	1	9	8	7	5

241

8	3	7	2	4	1	6	5	9
6	4	9	3	8	5	7	2	1
1	5	2	6	7	9	8	4	3
4	6	8	9	1	2	3	7	5
5	9	3	7	6	8	4	1	2
7	2	1	4	5	3	9	6	8
2	1	4	8	9	6	5	3	7
3	8	6	5	2	7	1	9	4
9	7	5	1	3	4	2	8	6

242

5	1	9	7	2	4	8	6	3
7	3	2	8	9	6	5	1	4
6	4	8	1	5	3	2	7	9
1	9	6	2	8	5	3	4	7
8	2	4	3	6	7	9	5	1
3	7	5	9	4	1	6	8	2
2	8	7	6	1	9	4	3	5
9	5	1	4	3	8	7	2	6
4	6	3	5	7	2	1	9	8

243

2	7	1	4	6	9	5	8	3
4	6	9	3	5	8	7	2	1
8	3	5	7	2	1	6	4	9
9	1	4	2	3	7	8	5	6
3	8	7	6	9	5	4	1	2
5	2	6	1	8	4	3	9	7
6	4	3	5	1	2	9	7	8
7	9	2	8	4	6	1	3	5
1	5	8	9	7	3	2	6	4

244

9	8	1	5	2	4	3	6	7
4	6	3	7	9	8	1	5	2
5	2	7	1	6	3	8	4	9
6	4	5	8	1	7	9	2	3
7	3	2	9	5	6	4	1	8
1	9	8	3	4	2	5	7	6
8	7	6	4	3	5	2	9	1
2	5	9	6	8	1	7	3	4
3	1	4	2	7	9	6	8	5

245

7	8	4	6	1	3	2	9	5
6	9	5	4	2	7	3	8	1
2	1	3	9	8	5	7	4	6
1	7	8	5	3	2	9	6	4
5	4	6	8	7	9	1	2	3
9	3	2	1	6	4	5	7	8
3	6	1	7	9	8	4	5	2
4	2	9	3	5	6	8	1	7
8	5	7	2	4	1	6	3	9

246

3	6	1	2	9	8	4	5	7
2	7	9	5	4	3	6	1	8
8	5	4	1	7	6	3	2	9
4	8	6	3	1	2	9	7	5
7	9	2	8	5	4	1	3	6
1	3	5	7	6	9	2	8	4
6	2	7	4	3	5	8	9	1
5	4	8	9	2	1	7	6	3
9	1	3	6	8	7	5	4	2

247

3	6	2	8	7	9	4	1	5
4	9	7	1	2	5	3	8	6
1	8	5	3	4	6	2	9	7
2	4	9	6	5	1	8	7	3
5	7	8	4	3	2	9	6	1
6	1	3	9	8	7	5	2	4
9	3	4	7	6	8	1	5	2
7	2	1	5	9	3	6	4	8
8	5	6	2	1	4	7	3	9

248

3	8	1	2	9	4	5	6	7
5	4	7	8	6	3	9	2	1
2	9	6	5	7	1	3	8	4
4	5	2	3	1	8	6	7	9
6	7	8	9	4	5	2	1	3
1	3	9	6	2	7	8	4	5
9	6	4	1	5	2	7	3	8
8	1	5	7	3	6	4	9	2
7	2	3	4	8	9	1	5	6

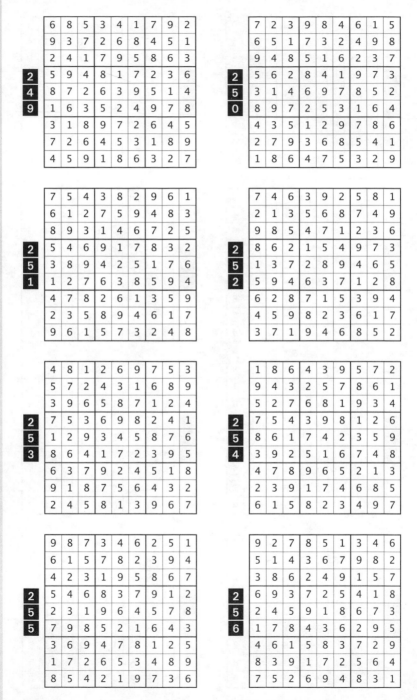

249

6	8	5	3	4	1	7	9	2
9	3	7	2	6	8	4	5	1
2	4	1	7	9	5	8	6	3
5	9	4	8	1	7	2	3	6
8	7	2	6	3	9	5	1	4
1	6	3	5	2	4	9	7	8
3	1	8	9	7	2	6	4	5
7	2	6	4	5	3	1	8	9
4	5	9	1	8	6	3	2	7

250

7	2	3	9	8	4	6	1	5
6	5	1	7	3	2	4	9	8
9	4	8	5	1	6	2	3	7
5	6	2	8	4	1	9	7	3
3	1	4	6	9	7	8	5	2
8	9	7	2	5	3	1	6	4
4	3	5	1	2	9	7	8	6
2	7	9	3	6	8	5	4	1
1	8	6	4	7	5	3	2	9

251

7	5	4	3	8	2	9	6	1
6	1	2	7	5	9	4	8	3
8	9	3	1	4	6	7	2	5
5	4	6	9	1	7	8	3	2
3	8	9	4	2	5	1	7	6
1	2	7	6	3	8	5	9	4
4	7	8	2	6	1	3	5	9
2	3	5	8	9	4	6	1	7
9	6	1	5	7	3	2	4	8

252

7	4	6	3	9	2	5	8	1
2	1	3	5	6	8	7	4	9
9	8	5	4	7	1	2	3	6
8	6	2	1	5	4	9	7	3
1	3	7	2	8	9	4	6	5
5	9	4	6	3	7	1	2	8
6	2	8	7	1	5	3	9	4
4	5	9	8	2	3	6	1	7
3	7	1	9	4	6	8	5	2

253

4	8	1	2	6	9	7	5	3
5	7	2	4	3	1	6	8	9
3	9	6	5	8	7	1	2	4
7	5	3	6	9	8	2	4	1
1	2	9	3	4	5	8	7	6
8	6	4	1	7	2	3	9	5
6	3	7	9	2	4	5	1	8
9	1	8	7	5	6	4	3	2
2	4	5	8	1	3	9	6	7

254

1	8	6	4	3	9	5	7	2
9	4	3	2	5	7	8	6	1
5	2	7	6	8	1	9	3	4
7	5	4	3	9	8	1	2	6
8	6	1	7	4	2	3	5	9
3	9	2	5	1	6	7	4	8
4	7	8	9	6	5	2	1	3
2	3	9	1	7	4	6	8	5
6	1	5	8	2	3	4	9	7

255

9	8	7	3	4	6	2	5	1
6	1	5	7	8	2	3	9	4
4	2	3	1	9	5	8	6	7
5	4	6	8	3	7	9	1	2
2	3	1	9	6	4	5	7	8
7	9	8	5	2	1	6	4	3
3	6	9	4	7	8	1	2	5
1	7	2	6	5	3	4	8	9
8	5	4	2	1	9	7	3	6

256

9	2	7	8	5	1	3	4	6
5	1	4	3	6	7	9	8	2
3	8	6	2	4	9	1	5	7
6	9	3	7	2	5	4	1	8
2	4	5	9	1	8	6	7	3
1	7	8	4	3	6	2	9	5
4	6	1	5	8	3	7	2	9
8	3	9	1	7	2	5	6	4
7	5	2	6	9	4	8	3	1

257

4	8	2	1	7	5	9	3	6
6	3	1	4	9	8	5	7	2
9	5	7	2	6	3	8	4	1
2	4	8	9	3	1	6	5	7
5	6	9	7	8	4	1	2	3
1	7	3	5	2	6	4	8	9
3	2	4	6	5	9	7	1	8
7	1	6	8	4	2	3	9	5
8	9	5	3	1	7	2	6	4

258

3	9	6	5	1	8	2	4	7
8	5	7	2	6	4	3	9	1
1	4	2	7	3	9	5	8	6
7	1	9	3	2	6	4	5	8
4	6	8	1	9	5	7	2	3
2	3	5	8	4	7	1	6	9
9	2	4	6	7	3	8	1	5
6	8	3	4	5	1	9	7	2
5	7	1	9	8	2	6	3	4

259

9	5	1	7	2	6	8	4	3
4	7	8	3	1	5	9	6	2
6	2	3	9	4	8	5	7	1
5	4	6	8	7	1	2	3	9
8	1	9	6	3	2	7	5	4
2	3	7	5	9	4	1	8	6
7	9	5	1	6	3	4	2	8
1	6	2	4	8	7	3	9	5
3	8	4	2	5	9	6	1	7

260

9	6	8	7	4	3	1	2	5
2	3	7	6	5	1	8	9	4
5	1	4	9	8	2	3	7	6
8	4	5	3	9	7	2	6	1
6	2	3	5	1	4	9	8	7
7	9	1	2	6	8	5	4	3
4	7	2	8	3	5	6	1	9
1	5	6	4	2	9	7	3	8
3	8	9	1	7	6	4	5	2

261

7	5	2	6	9	1	4	3	8
3	8	4	5	2	7	1	9	6
9	6	1	8	4	3	2	7	5
5	3	6	2	1	9	7	8	4
2	1	8	4	7	6	3	5	9
4	7	9	3	8	5	6	1	2
1	4	3	9	5	2	8	6	7
8	9	7	1	6	4	5	2	3
6	2	5	7	3	8	9	4	1

262

5	1	3	8	2	7	6	4	9
9	8	7	3	6	4	2	5	1
4	2	6	5	9	1	7	8	3
7	5	9	4	1	6	3	2	8
8	6	2	9	3	5	4	1	7
3	4	1	7	8	2	5	9	6
1	7	5	6	4	8	9	3	2
2	3	4	1	7	9	8	6	5
6	9	8	2	5	3	1	7	4

263

1	5	7	9	6	4	8	2	3
3	6	4	1	2	8	5	9	7
8	9	2	7	5	3	6	1	4
6	1	5	3	9	2	4	7	8
7	4	3	6	8	1	2	5	9
9	2	8	5	4	7	3	6	1
5	3	6	4	1	9	7	8	2
4	8	9	2	7	6	1	3	5
2	7	1	8	3	5	9	4	6

264

9	4	6	1	3	7	8	2	5
5	2	7	6	8	9	1	4	3
1	3	8	5	2	4	9	7	6
7	8	4	9	6	3	2	5	1
3	9	1	4	5	2	7	6	8
6	5	2	7	1	8	3	9	4
4	7	5	8	9	1	6	3	2
8	6	3	2	7	5	4	1	9
2	1	9	3	4	6	5	8	7

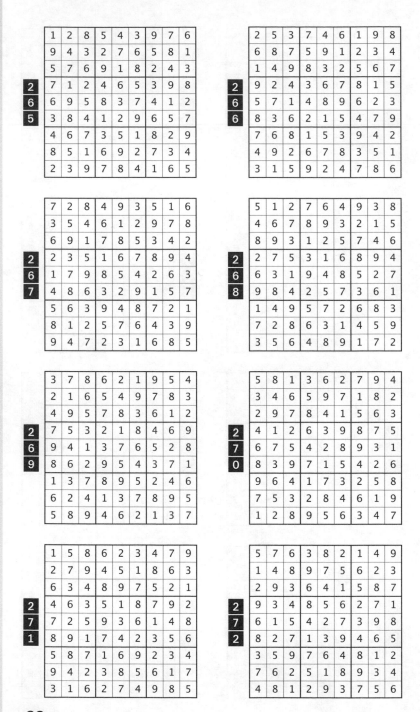

265

1	2	8	5	4	3	9	7	6
9	4	3	2	7	6	5	8	1
5	7	6	9	1	8	2	4	3
7	1	2	4	6	5	3	9	8
6	9	5	8	3	7	4	1	2
3	8	4	1	2	9	6	5	7
4	6	7	3	5	1	8	2	9
8	5	1	6	9	2	7	3	4
2	3	9	7	8	4	1	6	5

266

2	5	3	7	4	6	1	9	8
6	8	7	5	9	1	2	3	4
1	4	9	8	3	2	5	6	7
9	2	4	3	6	7	8	1	5
5	7	1	4	8	9	6	2	3
8	3	6	2	1	5	4	7	9
7	6	8	1	5	3	9	4	2
4	9	2	6	7	8	3	5	1
3	1	5	9	2	4	7	8	6

267

7	2	8	4	9	3	5	1	6
3	5	4	6	1	2	9	7	8
6	9	1	7	8	5	3	4	2
2	3	5	1	6	7	8	9	4
1	7	9	8	5	4	2	6	3
4	8	6	3	2	9	1	5	7
5	6	3	9	4	8	7	2	1
8	1	2	5	7	6	4	3	9
9	4	7	2	3	1	6	8	5

268

5	1	2	7	6	4	9	3	8
4	6	7	8	9	3	2	1	5
8	9	3	1	2	5	7	4	6
2	7	5	3	1	6	8	9	4
6	3	1	9	4	8	5	2	7
9	8	4	2	5	7	3	6	1
1	4	9	5	7	2	6	8	3
7	2	8	6	3	1	4	5	9
3	5	6	4	8	9	1	7	2

269

3	7	8	6	2	1	9	5	4
2	1	6	5	4	9	7	8	3
4	9	5	7	8	3	6	1	2
7	5	3	2	1	8	4	6	9
9	4	1	3	7	6	5	2	8
8	6	2	9	5	4	3	7	1
1	3	7	8	9	5	2	4	6
6	2	4	1	3	7	8	9	5
5	8	9	4	6	2	1	3	7

270

5	8	1	3	6	2	7	9	4
3	4	6	5	9	7	1	8	2
2	9	7	8	4	1	5	6	3
4	1	2	6	3	9	8	7	5
6	7	5	4	2	8	9	3	1
8	3	9	7	1	5	4	2	6
9	6	4	1	7	3	2	5	8
7	5	3	2	8	4	6	1	9
1	2	8	9	5	6	3	4	7

271

1	5	8	6	2	3	4	7	9
2	7	9	4	5	1	8	6	3
6	3	4	8	9	7	5	2	1
4	6	3	5	1	8	7	9	2
7	2	5	9	3	6	1	4	8
8	9	1	7	4	2	3	5	6
5	8	7	1	6	9	2	3	4
9	4	2	3	8	5	6	1	7
3	1	6	2	7	4	9	8	5

272

5	7	6	3	8	2	1	4	9
1	4	8	9	7	5	6	2	3
2	9	3	6	4	1	5	8	7
9	3	4	8	5	6	2	7	1
6	1	5	4	2	7	3	9	8
8	2	7	1	3	9	4	6	5
3	5	9	7	6	4	8	1	2
7	6	2	5	1	8	9	3	4
4	8	1	2	9	3	7	5	6

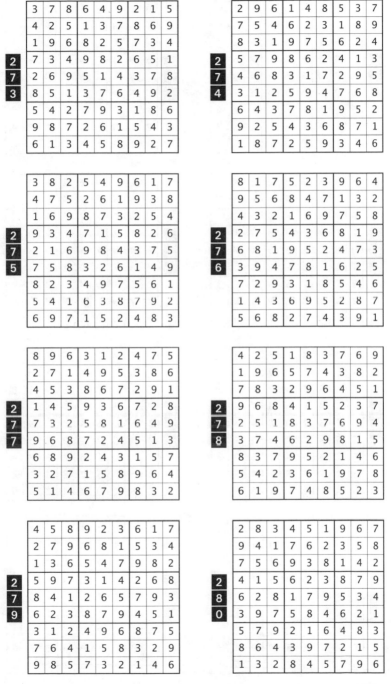

273

3	7	8	6	4	9	2	1	5
4	2	5	1	3	7	8	6	9
1	9	6	8	2	5	7	3	4
7	3	4	9	8	2	6	5	1
2	6	9	5	1	4	3	7	8
8	5	1	3	7	6	4	9	2
5	4	2	7	9	3	1	8	6
9	8	7	2	6	1	5	4	3
6	1	3	4	5	8	9	2	7

274

2	9	6	1	4	8	5	3	7
7	5	4	6	2	3	1	8	9
8	3	1	9	7	5	6	2	4
5	7	9	8	6	2	4	1	3
4	6	8	3	1	7	2	9	5
3	1	2	5	9	4	7	6	8
6	4	3	7	8	1	9	5	2
9	2	5	4	3	6	8	7	1
1	8	7	2	5	9	3	4	6

275

3	8	2	5	4	9	6	1	7
4	7	5	2	6	1	9	3	8
1	6	9	8	7	3	2	5	4
9	3	4	7	1	5	8	2	6
2	1	6	9	8	4	3	7	5
7	5	8	3	2	6	1	4	9
8	2	3	4	9	7	5	6	1
5	4	1	6	3	8	7	9	2
6	9	7	1	5	2	4	8	3

276

8	1	7	5	2	3	9	6	4
9	5	6	8	4	7	1	3	2
4	3	2	1	6	9	7	5	8
2	7	5	4	3	6	8	1	9
6	8	1	9	5	2	4	7	3
3	9	4	7	8	1	6	2	5
7	2	9	3	1	8	5	4	6
1	4	3	6	9	5	2	8	7
5	6	8	2	7	4	3	9	1

277

8	9	6	3	1	2	4	7	5
2	7	1	4	9	5	3	8	6
4	5	3	8	6	7	2	9	1
1	4	5	9	3	6	7	2	8
7	3	2	5	8	1	6	4	9
9	6	8	7	2	4	5	1	3
6	8	9	2	4	3	1	5	7
3	2	7	1	5	8	9	6	4
5	1	4	6	7	9	8	3	2

278

4	2	5	1	8	3	7	6	9
1	9	6	5	7	4	3	8	2
7	8	3	2	9	6	4	5	1
9	6	8	4	1	5	2	3	7
2	5	1	8	3	7	6	9	4
3	7	4	6	2	9	8	1	5
8	3	7	9	5	2	1	4	6
5	4	2	3	6	1	9	7	8
6	1	9	7	4	8	5	2	3

279

4	5	8	9	2	3	6	1	7
2	7	9	6	8	1	5	3	4
1	3	6	5	4	7	9	8	2
5	9	7	3	1	4	2	6	8
8	4	1	2	6	5	7	9	3
6	2	3	8	7	9	4	5	1
3	1	2	4	9	6	8	7	5
7	6	4	1	5	8	3	2	9
9	8	5	7	3	2	1	4	6

280

2	8	3	4	5	1	9	6	7
9	4	1	7	6	2	3	5	8
7	5	6	9	3	8	1	4	2
4	1	5	6	2	3	8	7	9
6	2	8	1	7	9	5	3	4
3	9	7	5	8	4	6	2	1
5	7	9	2	1	6	4	8	3
8	6	4	3	9	7	2	1	5
1	3	2	8	4	5	7	9	6

281

7	6	1	4	9	3	8	5	2
3	5	4	2	1	8	6	7	9
9	8	2	6	5	7	3	1	4
1	4	5	8	2	9	7	6	3
2	7	3	5	6	1	4	9	8
8	9	6	3	7	4	1	2	5
5	1	8	7	4	2	9	3	6
4	2	9	1	3	6	5	8	7
6	3	7	9	8	5	2	4	1

282

9	2	5	3	1	4	8	6	7
1	3	8	6	7	2	9	4	5
4	7	6	8	9	5	2	3	1
6	9	1	7	4	3	5	8	2
2	8	3	1	5	6	4	7	9
7	5	4	9	2	8	3	1	6
5	4	7	2	8	1	6	9	3
8	6	9	5	3	7	1	2	4
3	1	2	4	6	9	7	5	8

283

3	9	5	1	8	2	6	4	7
4	2	1	9	7	6	8	3	5
6	7	8	5	4	3	9	2	1
7	6	2	4	3	8	5	1	9
9	8	3	2	1	5	4	7	6
1	5	4	6	9	7	3	8	2
8	1	9	7	5	4	2	6	3
2	4	7	3	6	9	1	5	8
5	3	6	8	2	1	7	9	4

284

1	2	4	9	6	5	8	3	7
6	3	5	8	7	4	9	2	1
8	9	7	1	2	3	6	5	4
5	1	2	4	8	6	7	9	3
3	4	9	7	5	2	1	8	6
7	8	6	3	9	1	5	4	2
2	5	1	6	4	8	3	7	9
4	7	3	5	1	9	2	6	8
9	6	8	2	3	7	4	1	5

285

1	8	2	4	6	5	9	3	7
4	6	7	9	3	2	5	8	1
9	3	5	8	1	7	2	4	6
7	9	4	6	5	3	1	2	8
2	1	3	7	9	8	4	6	5
8	5	6	1	2	4	3	7	9
5	7	8	3	4	1	6	9	2
3	2	9	5	8	6	7	1	4
6	4	1	2	7	9	8	5	3

286

8	1	2	3	9	5	6	7	4
6	9	3	4	8	7	1	2	5
5	7	4	2	1	6	9	3	8
9	2	7	6	5	1	8	4	3
1	5	6	8	4	3	2	9	7
4	3	8	7	2	9	5	6	1
7	4	5	1	6	2	3	8	9
3	6	9	5	7	8	4	1	2
2	8	1	9	3	4	7	5	6

287

7	1	5	2	9	6	8	3	4
8	9	2	7	4	3	1	5	6
4	6	3	5	8	1	2	9	7
1	7	6	9	3	5	4	8	2
2	8	9	6	1	4	3	7	5
5	3	4	8	2	7	6	1	9
3	5	1	4	6	9	7	2	8
6	2	7	1	5	8	9	4	3
9	4	8	3	7	2	5	6	1

288

6	2	8	4	1	9	5	3	7
9	3	5	8	6	7	4	1	2
7	4	1	2	3	5	6	8	9
1	7	3	6	2	8	9	4	5
4	5	2	3	9	1	8	7	6
8	6	9	5	7	4	1	2	3
5	1	6	7	8	3	2	9	4
2	9	7	1	4	6	3	5	8
3	8	4	9	5	2	7	6	1

289

6	7	1	9	8	2	5	4	3
8	2	9	4	3	5	1	7	6
4	5	3	6	7	1	9	2	8
3	4	6	5	1	8	7	9	2
9	1	2	7	4	3	6	8	5
7	8	5	2	9	6	4	3	1
1	3	7	8	6	9	2	5	4
5	6	4	3	2	7	8	1	9
2	9	8	1	5	4	3	6	7

290

4	8	7	6	5	1	9	2	3
1	3	9	7	4	2	8	5	6
2	5	6	8	3	9	1	4	7
7	1	2	9	8	6	4	3	5
5	6	3	4	1	7	2	8	9
8	9	4	3	2	5	7	6	1
3	2	1	5	9	8	6	7	4
6	4	8	1	7	3	5	9	2
9	7	5	2	6	4	3	1	8

291

6	1	5	2	4	7	8	9	3
7	4	2	8	3	9	1	5	6
3	8	9	5	1	6	7	4	2
4	2	7	6	8	5	9	3	1
1	3	6	4	9	2	5	7	8
5	9	8	3	7	1	6	2	4
8	5	3	9	6	4	2	1	7
9	6	1	7	2	3	4	8	5
2	7	4	1	5	8	3	6	9

292

5	8	4	6	3	9	7	2	1
2	7	6	1	4	5	9	8	3
1	3	9	8	2	7	4	5	6
3	5	8	2	6	4	1	9	7
4	6	7	5	9	1	8	3	2
9	2	1	3	7	8	5	6	4
8	4	2	9	1	6	3	7	5
6	1	5	7	8	3	2	4	9
7	9	3	4	5	2	6	1	8

293

7	5	9	1	3	4	6	8	2
8	1	4	7	2	6	5	3	9
6	3	2	9	5	8	1	7	4
5	2	7	6	1	3	4	9	8
9	6	3	4	8	2	7	1	5
4	8	1	5	7	9	3	2	6
1	9	6	2	4	7	8	5	3
3	4	5	8	9	1	2	6	7
2	7	8	3	6	5	9	4	1

294

6	5	2	1	9	8	7	3	4
1	7	9	4	6	3	8	2	5
8	4	3	5	2	7	1	6	9
5	8	1	3	4	2	9	7	6
3	6	4	9	7	1	5	8	2
2	9	7	6	8	5	4	1	3
9	2	8	7	5	6	3	4	1
7	3	5	2	1	4	6	9	8
4	1	6	8	3	9	2	5	7

295

9	6	1	7	3	5	2	8	4
8	5	4	2	6	1	9	7	3
3	7	2	8	9	4	6	5	1
4	8	5	6	7	9	3	1	2
6	3	7	5	1	2	4	9	8
2	1	9	4	8	3	7	6	5
7	2	3	1	5	6	8	4	9
5	9	8	3	4	7	1	2	6
1	4	6	9	2	8	5	3	7

296

2	8	9	1	5	3	7	4	6
4	7	1	2	9	6	8	3	5
3	6	5	7	8	4	9	2	1
7	1	6	5	3	9	2	8	4
5	3	4	8	2	1	6	7	9
9	2	8	6	4	7	1	5	3
1	5	2	4	6	8	3	9	7
6	4	3	9	7	2	5	1	8
8	9	7	3	1	5	4	6	2

297

9	7	4	2	8	6	3	1	5
3	1	5	7	4	9	8	6	2
2	8	6	5	3	1	9	7	4
7	3	8	1	6	4	5	2	9
6	9	1	3	2	5	7	4	8
5	4	2	9	7	8	1	3	6
8	2	9	6	1	7	4	5	3
1	5	3	4	9	2	6	8	7
4	6	7	8	5	3	2	9	1

298

9	7	4	2	3	5	8	6	1
3	1	6	4	8	7	2	5	9
5	2	8	9	6	1	7	4	3
2	6	1	3	5	4	9	8	7
4	9	5	7	1	8	6	3	2
7	8	3	6	2	9	4	1	5
8	3	7	5	4	2	1	9	6
1	5	9	8	7	6	3	2	4
6	4	2	1	9	3	5	7	8

299

9	2	4	3	6	8	7	1	5
1	7	3	2	5	4	6	8	9
5	8	6	7	1	9	3	2	4
6	4	9	5	8	7	2	3	1
8	3	2	6	4	1	5	9	7
7	5	1	9	2	3	4	6	8
3	1	7	4	9	6	8	5	2
2	6	8	1	7	5	9	4	3
4	9	5	8	3	2	1	7	6

300

1	9	3	2	4	8	5	6	7
4	2	5	9	7	6	1	3	8
8	6	7	1	5	3	9	4	2
3	5	6	8	2	9	4	7	1
7	4	8	5	6	1	3	2	9
9	1	2	4	3	7	8	5	6
6	7	9	3	1	5	2	8	4
5	8	4	6	9	2	7	1	3
2	3	1	7	8	4	6	9	5